CW00642816

ZOROASTRIANISM

BY

JOHN W. WATERHOUSE

THE BOOK TREE
San Diego, California

Originally published
1934
by The Epworth Press
London

New material, revisions and cover
© 2006
The Book Tree
All rights reserved

ISBN 978-1-58509-281-9

Cover layout and design
by Toni Villalas

Published by
The Book Tree
P.O. Box 16476
San Diego, CA 92176
www.thebooktree.com

We provide fascinating and educational products to help awaken the public to new ideas and
information that would not be available otherwise.
Call 1 (800) 700-8733 for our *FREE BOOK TREE CATALOG*.

INTRODUCTION

This obscure and ancient religion is receiving more and more attention in modern times due to its claimed influence by scholars upon Christianity. This particular author, however, focuses upon the relationship between Zoroastrianism and Judaism, as he sets out to prove that Christianity did in fact receive influence from Zoroastrianism, but that it was transmitted through Judaism. This route of transmission allows the author to clearly show how Judaism itself was directly affected by Zoroastrainism during the Exilic Period, a time when these two faiths were existing in close proximity to one another. Chapters include Zoroaster Himself, The Mission and Ministry of the Prophet, The Scriptures of Zoroastrianism, Doctrine of God, Doctrine of Man, and Developments and Contacts.

Paul Tice

ZOROASTRIANISM

CONTENTS

EDITOR'S FOREWORD

THE quest for God is one in which all nations have shared. Call Him what they may, all peoples seek God, though they seek not as do we. Yet to understand both their unity with and differences from us must help to closer sympathy and respect. The purpose of this series is not critical nor apologetic, but rather is it descriptive. It is that of giving some account, by reference to the scriptures and great teachers of other religions, of the way in which the faiths of the world have faced the same spiritual issues that are ours. In this respect they are intended as a simply written contribution to the work of the Comparative Study of Religions.

E.S.W.

PREFACE

WHEN Gibbon wrote of the religion of Zoroaster, he apologized lest 'the studied obscurity of a prophet, the figurative style of the East, and the deceitful medium of a French or Latin version, may have betrayed us into error or heresy in this abridgement of Persian theology.' Anyone who tries, no matter in how humble a way, to describe a religion not his own, owes a like apology. The object of the book is descriptive, and the teaching of Zoroaster himself, rather than the later developments of the faith, has been kept in view. The writer feels that the Christian heritage through Judaism has been enriched by the Prophet of Iran, who, many centuries before the coming of Jesus Christ, prepared the way by proclaiming One God whose demand is ethical. Special reference is made in this book to the relationships between Judaism and Zoroastrianism, particularly during the Exilic period, when the two religions were brought into close contact.

The writer wishes to pay tribute to the outstanding contribution given to this field of study by James Hope Moulton. As a member of the College to which he once rendered such distinguished service, it is a great privilege to dedicate this work to his memory. It will be observed that the general position here taken is his. Dr. Moulton's translation of the Gathas and of the statements of the Greek authors concerning the Persians are taken from his Hibbert Lectures on *Early Zoroastrianism*. The translation of other

9

passages from the Avesta is from *The Sacred Books of the East*, with such alterations as more recent research has afforded.

This little book is sent out with the hope that a greater appreciation may be found for the faith which sent three wise men to Bethlehem.

J.W.W.

DIDSBURY COLLEGE, MANCHESTER,
           June, 1934.

ZOROASTRIANISM

CHAPTER I

ZOROASTER HIMSELF

GREAT religions are often the children of great geniuses. Zoroastrianism is no exception. Although the personality of its founder is shrouded in mystery, we may know enough of Zoroaster to rank him high in the goodly fellowship of the prophets. Legend and folklore have done their part in hiding from view the essential man, yet there remains a trustworthy kernel of evidence. Beyond all doubt, in ancient Iran some hundreds of years before the coming of the Christ, there arose a Prophet, whose life and teaching left indelible impression. Those, however, who have taken it upon themselves to deny the existence of most historical figures, do not stop short when they come to the case of Zoroaster. So able a man as the late J. M. Robertson endeavoured to prove that Jesus, the Buddha and Zoroaster, among many others, never lived.[1] It is unnecessary to say more on this than to point out that Robertson's attempt to dismiss Zoroaster has not affected those who are versed in Iranian scholarship. Only one scholar of distinction, as far as the present writer is aware, has shared the view that Zoroaster was a myth. That great Orientalist,

[1] Dr. Moulton wrote : ' I have myself indeed divined and published the argument by which Mr. Robertson's successors fifty years hence will irrefutably prove him a myth.' *The Teaching of Zarathushtra*, p. 70.

James Darmesteter, after spending long years of study
on the Avestan literature, at the end of his life changed
the views he had so ably defended, and proclaimed
that belief in the historical character of Zoroaster was
a mistake. It was unfortunate that this scholar did
not live to read the arguments of the opposition, or
adequately to explain his thesis.

The date of Zoroaster's lifetime and the original
place of his preaching are alike disputed. Yet,
however doubtful these facts of his life may be, to
deny his existence is to create far greater problems.
Whether the name Zoroaster was the Prophet's own
is uncertain : it is more likely to have been a title,
just as ' Christ ' or ' Buddha,' and meant ' High
Priest.' In the Zoroastrian Bible, the Avesta, the
name is Zarathushtra, and the form we have adopted
here is taken from the Latin ' Zoroastres,' which owes
its origin to a similar Greek spelling. We are reminded
that many English proper names have variant forms :
Professor Williams Jackson likens that of Wyclif
(Wycliff, Wycliffe, &c.). A name occasionally given
by the Avesta to the Prophet is Zarathushtrotemo—
that is, the greatest or highest Zarathushtra, and the
obvious deduction is that there existed a succession of
men who assumed this office. Professor Martin Haug,
in his *Essays on the Parsis,* argues for the existence of
several contemporaneous Zarathushtras, at whose
head the Prophet was placed. That they were of the
same period does not seem likely, except in a very
broad way. Yet the name Zarathushtra, or Zoroaster,
may have borne a similar connotation to the modern
Parsi term ' Dastur,' which signifies the spiritual
overseer of a large community. Thus the Zarathushtrotemo would be roughly equivalent to the ' Dastur-

i-Dasturan,' or Chief Priest of the Parsis. Sometimes
the name Spitama, a patronymic, is linked with that
of Zarathushtra in the Avesta. Spitama is likely to
have been a famous ancestor of the Prophet's who left
his name with the clan ; sometimes the Prophet bears
this name alone, which by derivation comes from a
verb meaning ' to be white.' Of the name Zarathushtra itself, etymology can make little, except
that the latter half of the word, -ushtra, means ' camel,'
whilst zar may mean ' to be old,' or ' to be fierce.'
This ancient title has never been satisfactorily explained, but a totemistic origin is just possible. At
any rate, the stamp of one personality, and that a
strong and noble one, is evident in the earliest narratives. Williams Jackson, however, says we have
in the name ' a title which the man retained as a
birthright even after he became famed as a spiritual
and religious teacher. The very fact of his retaining
this somewhat prosaic appellative testifies to a strong
personality ; Zoroaster remains a man and he is not
dubbed anew with a poetic title when later sanctifica-
tion has thrown a halo of glory about his head.'[1]

The date of Zoroaster is a matter of much conjecture.
Strangely enough, it cannot with any certainty be
ascertained within a period of some six hundred years.
This is not for lack of evidence, but by reason of the
conflicting nature of the evidence. Professor Geldner,
in the *Encyclopaedia Britannica*, maintains that if the
Gathas (the earliest part of the Avesta) reach back, as
is almost certain, to the lifetime of Zoroaster, we must
assign the Prophet to the fourteenth century B.C.
On the other hand, Williams Jackson argues with
much conviction for the medieval Persian tradition

[1] *Zoroaster the Prophet of Ancient Iran*, p. 14.

that Zoroaster was born in the seventh century B.C.
Although these two dates represent the extremes that
are countenanced by modern scholarship, some
Classical writers, whose position as historians cannot
be ignored, have given the amazing date of six thousand
B.C. Aristotle apparently held this mistaken view,
which cannot now be considered seriously. The explanation may be that Zoroaster's spiritual body, or
Fravashi, was believed to have dwelt with the Archangels of God for some thousands of years previous to
his physical birth. Such is the reason given by E. W.
West and others. Another very early date is given
by Xanthos of Lydia (470 B.C.), the first Greek writer
to mention Zoroaster, who placed him six hundred
years before the Trojan war—that is, about 1,800 B.C.
The Prophet is even claimed by a Babylonian historian,
Beroses, as the founder of a Babylonian dynasty in
2,000 B.C. Putting aside these early guesses, and
assuming the other extreme, we should find Zoroaster
a contemporary of some of the great Hebrew prophets.
Between the sixth and the eighth centuries B.C. God
raised up many noble men who purified religion, not
only in Israel or Iran, but in other parts of the world.
Gautama the Buddha was born in the sixth century,
and Lao-tsze belongs also to this era, being some fifty
years senior to Confucius who was born only seven
years after Gautama. The coincidences cannot be
pressed, but there seems at that period to have been
a fullness of the times which God used to speak to
men 'in divers manners and in divers places.' We
cannot regard this late date for Zoroaster with confidence, though it is not without evidence that must
be taken into account. For instance, the Bundahish,
a Pahlavi book which has derived much material from

lost Avestan literature, agrees with many Arabic traditions in placing the beginning of the Prophet's ministry 272 years before the death of Alexander the Great. Alexander died in 323 B.C., and thus we are taken to the beginning of the sixth century B.C. One difficulty, among many, that stands in the way of such a date is that the great Persian King, Darius Hystaspis (latter half of the sixth century B.C.) was, from the inscriptions of his reign, a Zoroastrian, or a worshipper of Ahura Mazdah, whom the Prophet had proclaimed as the one true God. The teaching of Zoroaster may have taken root quickly, or else it may have been that Darius was a devotee of the old unreformed Persian faith, that had for many generations worshipped Ahura Mazdah amongst other deities. The fact that the father of Darius was named Vishtaspa has been explained on the assumption that he was deliberately so called in honour of the great King Vishtaspa who was the patron of Zoroaster. If this be so, there is more reason for accepting the position that Cyrus was also a Zoroastrian, which is strongly defended by Professor Meyer.

It must be remembered that some of the writings of the Prophet himself are contained in the Avesta. This ' Bible ' of the Zoroastrian faith is likely to have been complete by about 400 B.C., though, of course, the Pahlavi works which have been incorporated into the Avesta are of much later date. A long period is required for the growth and canonization of the Avesta. It has been argued by Haug that since Zoroaster is called in Yasna IX, 14 ' famous in the Aryan home,' his followers must have believed him to have emigrated thence in the dim centuries of the past, with the Iranians and the Indians. But this

description may be ' poetical ' rather than ' historical,'
and it would be precarious to draw conclusions from
it, except that it strengthens our thesis of a very early
date for the Prophet. Professor James Hope Moulton's
theory will therefore be accepted. The Prophet was
an historical character, who lived something like a
thousand years before the advent of Christ. His date
cannot be far removed from the Vedic period, and it
is likely that the Gathas are a little later than the
Vedas. Incidentally, they share no small amount of
their teaching. The names of the kith and kin of
Zoroaster in the Gathas show us his circumstances
portrayed in just the way they would not be if he
were a myth. Even in the later Pahlavi traditions
there are too many ' pillar passages ' to make us
discredit them entirely. In the Gathas the traditions
concerning the Prophet are the more reliable because
the miraculous and the legendary are so obviously
absent, ' the absolutely simple and natural picture of
the Prophet, drawn with convincing unconsciousness
by his own hand in the main, gives us its own creden-
tials by the very impossibility of accounting for
inventions.'[1] We see the man Zoroaster, his family
and his friends, amongst whom outstands Vishtaspa
the patron king. The father of Zoroaster was
Pourushaspa (' with grey horses ') and his mother was
Dughdhova (' who has milked cows '). Their names
are not found in the Gathas, but occur frequently in
the later Books, and by reason of their commonplace
agricultural meaning are not likely to be mythological.
Who would invent such a name for the mother of a
great religious leader ? Yet some have held these
names to have been mythological figments, and

[1] Moulton : *Treasure of the Magi*, p. 11.

Moulton's reply to one such cannot be forgotten. Thomas Hyde, in his *Historia* equated Dughdhova with *Dodo* 'and favours us with a plate whereby we may recognize the bird. Mythologists might make capital out of this : I cheerfully present them with the hint.'[1] The final Gatha is a nuptial ode in honour of the Prophet's daughter Pourucista ('very thoughtful'). She was born subsequently to the Prophet's call to preach, and like the children of Isaiah, was given a name with a religious connotation—such being unique in the family of Zoroaster. As we shall see later, the Prophet laid much stress in his teaching on the value of Good Thought, and it would seem that Zoroaster wished his daughter to be a living emblem of his message.

We shall deal further with the Gathic portrait of Zoroaster and his message in the next chapter. For the present we will examine some of the traditions that have accrued around his person. Many of these, when viewed from a standpoint strictly historical, are next to worthless ; yet they must have their place in any account of the Prophet if we are to appreciate the exalted regard in which Zoroaster was held. Sometimes legend is as important as history, and not of least importance are the parallels which some of these Persian stories afford with the traditions of other faiths.

It was claimed that three thousand years before the Prophet's birth, a vision was given to men of the Fravashi or ideal image of the future Zarathushtra. The Dinkart, a late summary of the Avesta, tells of a miraculous Glory that shone round his destined mother. The whole earth welcomed the coming of the great

[1] *Early Zoroastrianism*, p. 82.

2

Prophet, and supernatural signs were given to mark the event. The evil Spirits fled into the underworld at the news of his birth. The Pahlavi writings record that a divine light shone round the house at the nativity of Zoroaster, just as the Apocryphal Gospels tell how the cave in which they claim Jesus to have been born was filled with supernatural light. Zoroaster has been called ' the laughing Prophet ' because there is a tradition that he laughed, and did not cry, when he was born. The so called ' Messianic ' Eclogue of Virgil presents a close parallel—' Incipe, parve puer, risu cognoscere matrem ' (Begin, little child, to greet thy mother with a smile). It may well have been that the poet knew of the Zoroastrian tradition, and wished the coming Deliverer to emulate it. The Zartusht Namah, another Pahlavi work, records ' as he left the womb he laughed ; the house was enlightened by that laughter ; his father was astonished at him, at his laughter and beauty and loveliness. He said in his heart, " This is the glory of God. Save this child, every infant born into the world has wept." ' [1] So it was that ' all who were unclean and evil were stung to the heart at that laughter.' The Zartusht Namah further tells of a king, by name Duransuram, who having heard of the wonders and miraculous powers of the child, determined, like Herod, to put to death a possible rival. When, however, he came to the child's cradle he beheld ' a face like the early spring, beaming with the glory of God.' When the child was lifted from the cradle, the king drew a dagger to slay him, but the king's hand was immediately withered by Ahura Mazdah. At fifteen, the boy

[1] Translation of the Zartusht Namah from John Wilson's *Religion of the Parsis*.

attained his majority, according to Persian custom,
and assumed the Kusti, or sacred girdle, which signi-
fied his having taken religious vows. Little further is
heard of Zoroaster for a number of years after that,
but we gather that he had left home and had begun
to prepare himself by travel and meditation for the
life which he foresaw would be his lot. Stories are
told of his compassion and kindness both to man and
beast, as he roamed from place to place. Later he
married, at a fairly early age, but was able to continue
his ascetic habits. The whole story of his life up to
the age of thirty, when he is said to have begun his
ministry, is fragmentary, though what there is to be
known has been ably collated by Professor Williams
Jackson, to whom we owe a debt for the only reliable
research that has been done in English on the matter
of these traditions.[1] The stories recorded, and apparently believed, by some of the Classical writers about
Zoroaster are preposterous. Pliny, for example, in-
forms us that the Prophet lived for twenty years in a
desert on cheese ! Porphyrius claimed that Zoroaster
inhabited a cave on the side of a mountain, which has
a little more to commend it, as there are other traditions telling of the Prophet's communing with
Ahura on a mountain. That the Prophet received his
message from God in such a way is likely, for after
certain visions of God (see ch. II) he was called to set
out on a ministry of reformation of the old cult, and
to preach One God, whose first claim on man was
ethical. But bitter disappointment marked the early
preaching of Zoroaster. Men were indifferent to his
message, and it was ten years before he made his

[1] For this chapter generally, see Jackson: *Zoroaster the Prophet
of Ancient Iran.*

first convert, strangely enough one of his own family, Maidyoimaongha his cousin, who has been called ' the St. John of Zoroastrianism.' After this, the work of the Prophet began to prosper, and in a couple of years he was to win to his teaching King Vishtaspa of Seistan, the ruler of a large part of the country now known as Afghanistan. That such a man of influence favoured Zoroaster was of extreme importance to the whole history of the Persian faith, and apart from him Zoroaster might never have effected his mission. ' As the royal patron of Zoroaster and promoter of his cause,' says Dr. A. S. Geden, ' the King Vishtaspa occupies a somewhat similar relation to Zoroastrianism as is held by Asoka towards Buddhism, or Constantine to Christianity. The real history, however, of his life and reign is obscure and involved in legendary details and extravagancies.'[1] But of his actual existence there is no doubt, and the Gathas record not merely the name of Vishtaspa, but also the names of various members of his family.

Certain Persian traditions tell of the Prophet's visiting India, China and Turkey, but such distant journeyings are improbable, though he travelled widely. In the meanwhile Zoroaster received further confirmation of his ' call,' chiefly by way of visions. He now knew that God was the First and the Last— ' I conceived of thee, O Mazdah, in my thought that thou, the First, art (also) the Last—that thou art Father of Good Thought, for thus I apprehended thee with mine eye—that thou didst truly create Right, and art the Lord to judge the actions of life ' (Ys. XXXI, 8). Zoroaster then realizes that he must go to the priests (Mobeds) themselves, and bid them cast

[1] *Studies in the Religions of the East*, p. 689.

aside their evil practices. He must proclaim the protection of all good animals, especially those that are useful to agriculture. One tradition, of late origin, is that an Angel appeared to the Prophet and commanded him to take a message to the king Vishtaspa, that to the king had been committed the care of all the Fire Temples, but it is doubtful whether Zoroaster ever interested himself greatly in the ritual side of religion : his concern was prophetic rather than priestly. Subsequent ' commissions ' were given to Zoroaster and as he became increasingly certain of his faith he undertook the most difficult of tasks in preaching to another priestly caste, the Kavis, who were also governors of the land. But just as Amaziah drove Amos the prophet from Bethel, Zoroaster was driven away from the shrines by the priests, and wandered for a long while from place to place with scant success. He then had to undergo a period of temptation. The story of this is not recorded in the Gathas, but is told by the Dinkart, the Vendidad, the Zartusht Namah and the Dadistan, and probably reflects a real experience of the inner life of the Prophet. But Ahura had armed Zoroaster with a sacred formula, the Ahuna Vairya (which Williams Jackson calls ' the paternoster ' of Zoroastrianism), by the efficacy of which he had strength to meet all evil suggestions. The Vendidad (Ch. XIX) tells how the evil Spirit, Angra Mainyu, tempted the Prophet to ' curse the good religion of the worshippers of Mazdah and obtain a boon.' Zoroaster makes a noble reply : ' No, I shall not renounce the good religion of the worshippers of Mazdah, not though life and limb and soul should part asunder.' Whether Zoroaster would resort to spells, seeing that he preached against them, is more than doubtful, but as Moulton has observed, his followers revenged themselves by making his own words into spells.

The story of the conversion of Vishtaspa is told with much colour and little reliability by the Zartusht Namah and other late Books such as the Zatsparam. It is probable that the Prophet's advocacy of agriculture made first appeal to Vishtaspa, rather than his religious doctrines. The Dinkart states that it was on the royal racecourse that Zoroaster obtained first audience with the king. The Zartusht Namah paints a vivid picture of the jealousy aroused among the court magicians and wise men when Zoroaster found favour with the king. They plotted to take his life, informing the king that Zoroaster's power was in forbidden magic, and the Prophet was cast into prison. But as with all good stories of heroes and villains, there is a happy ending. The favourite horse of the king fell sick. None of the wise men or physicians of the court were able to restore the creature to health, but Zoroaster, released temporarily from his cell, achieved a seeming miracle on the animal, and obtained a high place in the palace. The Gathas give a more reliable account of the Prophet's activities at the court, and suggest that the teaching of Zoroaster found gradual acceptance among all the king's *entourage*. Whatever be the circumstances of the conversion of Vishtaspa, the king seems to have become a whole-hearted supporter of the ideals of the Prophet, and endeavoured to propagate this new teaching among his peoples. Wherever the reformation was resisted, Vishtaspa advanced with the sword, and the Prophet does not seem to have disagreed with this practice of ' holy war.'

Missionaries are said to have been sent from Iran to such distant parts as Hindustan. Says Williams Jackson, ' The claim to Indian converts is quite persistent in the later writings, which is not strange when we consider the Indo-Iranian kinship and the fact that the Parsis found in India an asylum from Mohammedan persecution.'[1] It is probable that Zoroaster ceased his own missionary travels when he had found footing at the court, though there are stories of his visiting Babylon. He taught, healed and preached for many years, and spent much time in the organization of the practical foundations of the reformation. But the religious antagonism the new faith evoked amongst neighbouring peoples was coming to a head, and, according to tradition, broke out in the Prophet's lifetime.

The Gathas do not record the wars that ensued, but this does not prove their legendary character, as might be supposed, for the Gathas are but fragments of a larger literature. The chief foes of Vishtaspa were the Turanians, under a famous leader Arjasp, or in full, Arjat-aspa. Moulton accounts for this hostility as being largely that of the eternal conflict between agriculturists and nomads, rather than being of essentially political origin. The Pahlavi writings speak of this conflict as ' the war of the religion.' The fact that Vishtaspa had refused to pay tribute to Arjasp became the bone of contention. Zoroaster himself had advised Vishtaspa not to pay the money, because Arjasp had refused to accept the new faith. Arjasp in his turn sends a message to Vishtaspa, that if he does not abandon the strange creed he has adopted, war would ensue. We have no reliable account of

[1] *Zoroaster the Prophet of Ancient Iran*, p. 85.

the battles fought in the struggle that followed, though they are described with much colour in the late Pahlavi work, the Shah Namah. Amongst the most distinguished warriors for the faith, however, is Vishtaspa's son, Isfendiar, who had come under the influence of the Prophet at the court. Isfendiar was largely instrumental in winning the first campaign, and was subsequently entrusted with a picked army with which to carry the flag of the reformation into distant parts of the Empire. But false stories were told to Vishtaspa concerning his son, who was compelled to resign his command, and the whole army became disorganized. Arjasp was quick to take this opportunity of striking another blow at Vishtaspa, and captured his capital, Balkh, whilst the king was absent in Seistan.

Tradition has it that Zoroaster was in Balkh at that time, and was struck down by the sword as he was doing duty at the Fire Temple of Nush-Adar. Vishtaspa returned home with speed, on hearing the news, and raised another army under the leadership of another son ; but this son, Farshidvard, was killed, and the army defeated. As a last resource, Isfendiar was released from the prison into which he had been cast, and made commander of a new force. Thereupon followed a complete reversal of the fortunes of Vishtaspa. Such a victory was won for the faith that its foundations were established securely for many years. Arjasp was killed, and his capital stormed. But Zoroaster, like many another prophet, had died when all seemed lost.

CHAPTER II

THE MISSION AND MINISTRY OF THE PROPHET

So far we have dealt with the bare outline of tne Prophet's life. We now consider the tasks to which he was called, and the way in which he faced them. We know very little of what preceded Zoroaster, or of the state of life and religion in ancient Persia. It would thus be difficult to estimate the Prophet's work alongside that of other men of genius, the conditions of whose lives are known. Zoroaster belongs to the dim background of history; yet the light of his personality has penetrated the years. For lack of evidence it is not possible to study him scientifically; yet our estimate of him is by no means hypothetical, and the great religion that evolved from his ministry is a monument to his own greatness. He is all the more to be honoured since he stands alone as a spiritual pioneer in a dark age : he came ' as one born out of due time,' for he was centuries ahead of his religious contemporaries in Iran. Even to-day, there are probably few Zoroastrians who would not admit that he is still ahead of the most eminent Parsi thinkers, for he had an immediate experience of God, and such an experience cannot be gained through mere learning or thought. The Prophet was not, it seems, a man of great learning, but a man of great vision and practical

understanding. He related religion to everyday life,
and had a message for all. Although he made appeal
to such men as the royal Vishtaspa, his words were
welcome to the humble folk who heard him gladly as
the champion of the struggling peasant classes. He
was a sufficiently noble-minded man to forget himself
in his work for others, and unlike many men of genius,
was no egoist. It is remarkable how his own personality and doings are obscured in his own writings—
the Gathas. Moulton is bold to say that ' in his poems
he contrives to suppress his personality more than
any other religious genius known to history.'[1] Some
of these Gathas are now lost, but enough remain to
indicate the scope of Zoroaster's mission and ministry.

The birthplace of the Prophet was probably in the
West of Iran ; yet this was not the scene of his
ministry, which seems to have been exercised in the
Eastern districts. Thither lay the domains of
Vishtaspa in Seistan, and there Zoroaster stayed
during the latter part of his life. The people whose
life he shared were divided into three main strata of
society—priests, warriors and peasants. These class
distinctions, however, are not so marked in the Gathas
as they are in the later Avesta : the state of society
in the Prophet's day was formative and transitional.
The majority of people to whom Zoroaster preached
were agriculturalists, whose mainstay was cattle
breeding. This kind of farming did not necessitate a
regular mode of life, and only in the later Books do
we find emphasis on the importance of the settled
industries, such as metal-working. It is significant
that one of the king's titles in the early days was
' Yima,' or ' having many sheep.' The Gathas show

[1] *Early Religious Poetry of Persia*, p. 39.

the original struggle between the two factions of the ancient Aryan people, the nomads and the would-be settlers. In fact, the whole Avesta is a commentary on a conflict which did not cease for many centuries. Because of danger of invasion from marauding bands, the settlers had constantly to take up the sword in self-defence. Thus from the Prophet's time onwards there was little pacifism in the Zoroastrian creed, and those who kept the faith had to fight hard to save it from sheer extinction.

Zoroaster came to a religious people, but their zeal was not according to knowledge. In the main, they were Nature worshippers, doing obedience to the ancient Aryan deities. The stage had not yet been reached when they could clearly distinguish between the deity itself and that in which the deity was believed to reside. Thus their worship of ' Father Heaven ' and ' Mother Earth,' and Mithra, the god of the rain and the sun. E. E. Kellett holds that most of these gods had not yet assumed ' proper ' names, and in the time of Zoroaster they were hardly personified. This is likely, though we cannot accept Kellett's point of view that the Prophet succeeded in turning popular mythology into a system as complicated as the world has known. Indeed, there is very little ' system ' in the teaching of Zoroaster himself ; his followers and interpreters have, however, made good this lack. Surely, too, if more of the writings of the Prophet had been preserved, his ' system ' might appear a little less complicated, and many references which are at present obscure might prove of easy interpretation.

Religion was, therefore, in the ' animistic ' stage when the Prophet appeared. In so far as society as well as religion was in a transitional state, Zoroaster's work was the easier. He had not to combat the rigid traditions that have broken so many of the great reformers. Neither had he to proclaim a new god, but to preach the exclusion of all other gods save Ahura. There may have been other prophets who had acted as forerunners to his preaching—for the work of a famous man is often dependent on the preparation made by men unknown—but we know nothing of them. The atmosphere into which the Prophet came has been called ' potentially monotheistic ' ; if this were so, Zoroaster was quick to harness the tide of the times. He proclaimed One God with no uncertain voice, and demanded a reform systematic and thorough. He spake as one with authority, for he felt he had been commissioned not from men, but of God. In the belief that he alone had been set aside by Ahura for a great task, he counted all others who claimed divine prerogatives to be men of falsehood—' I was ordained at the first by thee : all others I look upon with a spirit of hatred ' (Ys. XLIV, 11). With this consciousness of special mission, Zoroaster believed that his word was final and authoritative : those who disobeyed it would suffer, ' those of you that put not in practice this word as I think and utter it, to them shall be woe at the end of life,' but ' in eternity shall the souls of the righteous be joyful ' (Ys. XLV, 3, 7). In the Gathas there are many ' hard ' passages such as the above, but the sternness of the Prophet's words are best understood if we remember it was born out of the conviction that Ahura had revealed a message which was of ' life and death ' importance.

Zoroaster was more than a mere reformer setting out to improve the conditions of his land. He had

heard a call from God and had answered : ' Thou
didst tell me, go and teach Right, and thou didst not
command what I did not obey ' (Ys. XLIII, 12).
He does not work for the sake of man, though his
appeal is to man, and he is deeply moved by the lot
of the oppressed classes. Because of the great practical issues that confronted the Prophet, he delved
little into theological speculation : he was too pre-
occupied. The theological statements of the Gathas
may be summed up in the creed that Ahura the
creator is One, and that his demands are ethical.
But, simple as they may seem, to have reached what
is now known as ' ethical monotheism ' was a wonderful
achievement, and one which other faiths have been
slow to attain. Because Zoroaster was convinced
that God must be just, as he loved Asha (Truth,
Right), he had to face the great problem of the existence
and power of evil in the world. The Prophet felt that
Ahura must supply him with an answer to this. He
wrestled with the problem so long and realized the
fact of suffering so vividly that he personified evil.
But alongside of this, the conviction was given that
right and justice for the individual must ultimately
prevail, and so came to him an assurance of personal
immortality. Zoroaster, unlike many Easterns, felt
that the universe must be essentially rational, that
the mind of man was capable of comprehending
something of the sure purpose, waiting to be revealed
to the creation, in the mind of its creator. Thus
Zoroaster appealed to Ahura for answers to the
questions that perplexed him : one of the Gathas
(Ys. XLIV) gives a list of some nineteen queries so
put by the Prophet. What, he asks, is the reward
of the blessed, how is one to pray, who made light

and darkness, who yoked swiftness to winds and
clouds, what artist made sleep and waking, was his
own message indeed the truth and would men observe
it, on which side was the enemy ?

The Prophet makes little of the difficulty of finding
God : he speaks as one who has been ¹ ˙
of God. This consciousness was de
discipline which characterized espec
part of Zoroaster's life, but he seem
have relied on fasting or other exter
way of producing trances or ecsta
God had first spoken, and the Prop
In some passages in the Gathas, ho
calls himself a ' knower.' This word
some of the significance associated wit
ties of the ancient visionary, but her   y to
have meant little more than ' one w.—.s initiated
into the laws of Ahura.' It is certainly not a claim
for exclusive knowledge not lawful to other men,
though, as we have seen, Zoroaster considered himself
to have been exclusively separated by God for a special
task. It was his experience, rather than his com-
mission, which the Prophet felt others could share.
In this experience, moreover, there was little of the
mystical, except in so far as any direct consciousness
of God's workings may merit this term. With Zoroaster
there were associated none of the repulsive elements
that are so often found in conjunction with Eastern
mysticism : he knew that the hand of God could be
discerned in the ordinary realm of phenomena. The
following important words occur frequently in the
Gathas : ' As the Holy One I recognized thee, O
Mazdah Ahura.' Whether this refers to one experience or to several is not clear, but this recognition was

probably consequent on prayer, and there is no indication of any abnormal state of mind. The Prophet records that he stretched forth his hands, as was the custom of the Persians, in the attitude of prayer. The first of the extant Gathas thus begins : ' With outspread hands in petition for that help, O Mazdah, first of all things will I pray for the works of the holy spirit ' (Ys. XXVIII, 1). In this communion between Ahura the creator and Zoroaster his prophet, they speak ' face to face.' There is little emphasis upon the ' otherness ' of God, or on the majesty of the presence of Ahura, who is nevertheless regarded as all-powerful. In one Gathic passage, the Prophet asks for the help of Ahura ' as friend gives to friend.' Whether this should be claimed as representative of Zoroaster's attitude to Ahura, however, is doubtful, as the Gatha in question is an early one, reflecting the struggles of the Prophet to gain a footing in the land. A very human preacher exclaims ' I know wherefore I am without success, Mazdah : (because) few cattle are mine, and for that I have but few folk. I cry unto thee, see thou to it, Ahura, granting me support as friend gives to friend ' (Ys. XLVI, 2).

Much of the spiritual history of the Prophet is enshrined in the Gathas, and we can see that he endured travail of soul and body before he embarked on his ministry. In fact, this struggle did not cease even after Vishtaspa became Zoroaster's wealthy patron, for besides the wars and rumours of wars, the Prophet never seems to have felt assured of the ultimate acceptance of his message. Originally, moreover, he had endured something of the hard fortunes of those for whose betterment he had been sent to work. Thus Zoroaster rises to his heights when dealing with such things as social oppression and the abuse of husbandry. One of his prayers (Ys. XLV, 9) is sufficient example of this—' May Mazdah Ahura by his dominion bring us to work, for prospering our beasts and our men, so that we may through Right have familiarity with Good Thought.' The reference to the lot of the cattle, in the above Gatha, is especially significant. Although the Prophet protested chiefly against lack of true husbandry, and against sacrifices in which blood was shed, he made strong outcry against the cattle-stealing expeditions of the nobles, who were the robber-barons of those days. There is no reason to think that the cow or the ox were regarded as too sacred to be killed for food, as Hinduism holds ; one of the Yasnas commands that the cow shall be fattened for food. The high regard for cattle is largely due to the fact that the number of beasts a man possessed was the chief measure of his wealth and means of his livelihood, as in Old Testament days.

The Ox-Soul (Geush Urvan) as thus representing agriculture, was personified, and had a place in the heavenly council of Ahura Mazdah. There it had cried out ' For whom did ye fashion me ? Who created me ? Violence and rapine hath oppressed me, and outrage and might. I have no other herdsman than you (Ahura) : prepare for me then the blessings of pasture ' (Ys. XXIX, 1). Then the Ox-Creator[1] inquires of the Right (Asha), ' Hast thou a judge (Ratu) for the Ox. . . . Whom do ye will to be his lord, who may drive off violence together with the followers of the Lie ? ' (verse 2). Asha replies, ' There

[1] Moulton thinks this was Mithra, but Söderblom names Ahura himself.

is for the Ox no helper that can keep harm away. Those (men) yonder have no knowledge how right-doers act towards the lowly ' (verse 3). Then Good Thought (Vohu Manah) whose special care is over the beasts of the field, declares that Zoroaster is fitted to be the protector of cattle—' He is known to me who alone hath heard our commands, even Zarathushtra Spitama : he willeth to make known our thoughts, O Mazdah, and those of the Right. So let us bestow on him charm of speech ' (verse 8).

With the assurance of this vocation and gift, the Prophet proclaimed the care of cattle as a sacred and religious duty, which has been honoured throughout Persian history. Zoroaster regarded his message as a ' manthra,' which in later usage came almost to mean a ' spell,' but to him it certainly did not mean that, although, as we have just seen, he was conscious that there had been bestowed on him a unique ' charm of speech.' It was the purpose of the Prophet that men should themselves perceive the ' rationale ' of his teaching and reform, which was of an extremely practical nature. He had made concrete and understandable many of the theological conceptions of his day. For instance, in order to illustrate the idea of the Kingdom of God, he had likened it to a beautiful meadow, and the ox, as being the farmer's hope, was made another name for Paradise. Nevertheless, we cannot deny that there was a certain very indefinite element in the teaching of Zoroaster. The Prophet had avoided the majority of those anthropomorphic conceptions which would facilitate the picture of God in the mind of the ordinary man. It seems that he took away many popular ideas, some of which he made no attempt to replace. In the Gathas there is not

3

even mention of the deities which must have held men's devotion then, as later. Mithra, Anahita and the Fravashis are conspicuous by their absence. We should desire some teaching from the Prophet on their nature and position in his system : it is possible that he relegated some of these ancient deities to the realm of the evil spirits. Yet the gods and goddesses were soon to be re-enthroned, and before many years had passed there was great need for another reformation. One feels that such would not have been necessary had Zoroaster left more definite teaching on the implications of his creed. In holding up the truth, Zoroaster had believed that the untrue would perish, but men were not ready to receive so high a teaching : once again, we see the Prophet had come before the time was ripe. It may naturally be replied that the Gathas are but a small portion of his teaching, in fact, just a few of his poems, and that arguments built from silence are seldom the strongest. The fact, however, remains that not sufficient of Zoroaster's own doctrine was handed down for Parsism to have any real conception of that for which its great Prophet had lived and died to witness. The cornerstone of the later faith was made of that which Zoroaster had rejected.

Zoroaster must have hoped that with the powerful aid of King Vishtaspa, and the forceful missionary activity that radiated from his capital, and by the ' holy wars ' that were waged to establish the standard of the faith in distant lands, he would claim the East in allegiance to his teaching. But this was never to be. Many reasons could be given for the failure, but Archbishop Söderblom has pointed out the most significant—Zoroaster had not pondered sufficiently long and deeply over the ultimate purposes of life. In his estimate of life, moreover, the Prophet had not realized that the greatest battles are fought within the heart of man, and that the worst enemy a man has to fight is himself. The chief enemies Zoroaster set himself to oppose were external ones, and not by the conquest of these can peace of soul or real victory in life be gained : ' the conquest of self never entered into his ethical programme. The art of overcoming evil with good remained unknown to him. He declared on the contrary that he who is good to an evil person becomes evil himself and worthy of punishment ' (Ys. XLVI, 6).[1] Such a doctrine seems strange in these days, but Zoroaster had not learned to hate the sin and love the sinner. The Prophet's theory of punishment is crude, and for him there is no ' Golden Rule.' Although it was the will of Ahura that the faithless should turn to him, anyone who inflicted punishment on the ungodly rendered service to the creator—' Whoso worketh ill for the liar by word or thought or hands, or converts his dependent to the good, such men meet the will of Ahura Mazdah to his satisfaction ' (Ys. XXXIII, 2). Nevertheless, Zoroaster had a fine conception of moral obligation. The implication of some of his ideas, however, had not been sufficiently considered. Although Zoroaster did unique work in linking ethics with religion, he had assumed for the most part the ethics of his time. The result would have been more satisfactory had the Prophet more closely scrutinized the standards he adopted. For example, Zoroaster accepted the axiom of the day, that force must be met with force : he did not realize the power of love to cast out wrong. To be on

1 N. Söderblom: *The Living God*, p. 211.

the side of Ahura meant resistance of any nature to
all evil, the more vigorous the better. All followers
of the Druj, or Falsehood, together with all sorcerers
and magicians, were the enemies of those who had
acknowledged Ahura. The faithful won his especial
favour by tending their lands, looking after their flocks
and herds, and forsaking the nomadic life which was
not profitable to the welfare of the State. This ideal
was upheld through centuries of development in
ancient Persia, and even the Vendidad (third century
B.C.) takes up again the Prophet's emphasis on
agriculture, in the following vivid form :

> When the corn is prepared, the devils sweat.
> When the mill is prepared, the devils despond.
> When the meal is prepared, the devils howl.
> When the dough is prepared, the devils are done for.
> (Fargard 3.) [1]

Gibbon, in his *Decline and Fall*,[2] writes with admiration for the social teaching of Zoroaster, and cites
with approval this interest in agriculture, which he
illustrates from a passage in the Avesta : ' He who
sows the ground with care and diligence acquires a
greater stock of merit than he could gain by the
repetition of ten thousand prayers.' Such a saying is
true to the spirit of the Prophet, even if not coming
from his lips. In fact, in the Gathas themselves there
is no mention of sowing or reaping. We gather from
this that there was little settled agriculture carried
on in the early times, and that the keeping of stock
was then the main occupation of the farmers of Iran.
Söderblom, however, finds explanation of this lack of
mention of tilling by reason of the fact that in certain
parts of the Bernese Oberland the presence of grazing

1 Söderblom's translation.
2 Vol. I, ed. William Smith, p. 336.

cattle on clean, prepared pasturage, allows of culti-
vation of crops without tillage of the soil. Similar
conditions and methods may possibly have obtained
in Zoroaster's day, but the assumption is precarious,
especially as the theory does not account for the
absence of mention of sowing.

Zoroaster's demands did not allow for difference of
privilege between rich and poor. The Prophet looked
on all men alike, except that he seems to have divided
them up mentally into two rigid divisions of good
and bad, irrespective of class distinctions. Although
he became champion of the poor, it was not merely
because they were poor. He was not concerned with
the usual disputes between the aristocracy and the
working man. Justice was his chief concern. If the
agricultural classes had been in the wrong, we feel
that Zoroaster would have decried them as vehemently
as he denounced the nobles. In fact, he himself
belonged to the upper classes which he condemns, and
the only way in which relief for the poor could be
effected was by means of the very people he attacked.
Zoroaster was a priest, and in one of the Yasnas
describes himself as such : ' I, as a Priest (Zaota),
who would learn the straight (paths) by the Right,
would learn by the Best Spirit how to practice husbandry ' (Ys. XXXIII, 6). In him, therefore, we
have a strange combination of priest and prophet.
It is possible that in his earlier days, Zoroaster had
been one of the Karapans, an order of priests which
receives special condemnation in the Gathas, perhaps
because the Prophet had inside knowledge of their
practices.

With the Karapans are linked, in the Gathas, the
Kavis, who were the chiefs of the land. Apparently

they governed oppressively, and consequently gained
the reputation of being ' followers of the Druj.' Curi-
ously enough, the title Kavi belonged to the dynasty
of which Vishtaspa was a member. But, as patron
of the faith, the Kavi Vishtaspa is of course exempt
from indictment in the Gathas, and proves the exception to the rule. The Kavis and the Karapans were
in alliance against the Prophet, and one of the Yasnas
tells of an insult Zoroaster received at the hands of a
priest who would not give him shelter on a journey
one cold night. Zoroaster rankled at the memory :
' The Kavi's wanton did not please Zarathushtra at
the Winter Gate, in that he stayed him from taking
refuge with him, and when there came to him also
Zarathushtra's two steeds shivering with cold ' (Ys.
LI, 12). For this and other misdeeds, says the
Prophet, the priests and nobles shall not escape
punishment, if not in this life, in the next. When
they shall try to cross the Bridge that leads to Paradise,
they will be confronted with the vision of their own
wickedness, and be taken down to Hell—' By their
dominion the Karapans and the Kavis accustomed
mankind to evil actions, so as to destroy life. Their
own soul and their own self shall torment them when
they come to the Bridge of the Separater. To all
time they shall be guests for the House of the Lie '
(Ys. XLVI, 11). Apparently these Kavis and Karapans made use of the Haoma, an intoxicating drink
which Zoroaster would not allow. The taking of it
was supposed to confer immortality on the drinker,
and no doubt its effect would result in a kind of
religious frenzy. Thus the Prophet wrote : ' To his
(Zoroaster's) undoing, Grehma (one of the leaders of
the opposition to the reform) and the Kavis have long

devoted their purposes and energies, for they set themselves to help the liar, and that it may be said " The Ox shall be slain, that it may kindle the Averter of Death to help us." Thereby hath come to ruin the Karapan and the Kavi community . . .' (Ys. XXXII, 14-15). Zoroaster had a great loathing for the Haoma, and cries to Ahura ' When wilt thou smite the filthiness of this intoxicant through which the Karapans evilly deceive ? ' (Ys. XLVIII, 10). But he never succeeded in abolishing it, as the later history of the Parsis abundantly shows.

Other enemies of the Prophet were especially the worshippers of the Daevas. The Daevas were the ancient Aryan deities which had been adopted by the nomads as patrons of their cattle-raiding exploits. Their name had originally no evil significance, and is cognate etymologically with the word ' Deus,' &c., but the Turanians who worshipped the Daevas had caused evil associations for the Iranian mind. As has been previously suggested, the nomadic Turanians, who lived in the north-east of Persia, were no friends of the inhabitants of Iran, and their scorn of agriculture had caused hostility between the two peoples, although in blood relationship they were closely akin. The Turanians are, however, mentioned once with favour in the Gathas, as some of them seem to have embraced the faith of the Prophet: yet these must have been very few. Tiele has likened the conflict between the adherents of Jehovah and the Baalim to the above struggle. Yet, as Söderblom has aptly pointed out, the analogy is not entirely satisfactory, because a certain difference had existed ' ab initio ' between the worshippers of Jehovah and those of Baal, but the Turanians and the Zoroastrians had both originated from the same stock.

A further word must be said concerning the moral teaching of the Prophet, the sanity of which can hardly be over-estimated. It has, in fact, been claimed that no ancient religion was more bound up with morality than was Zoroastrianism. Says Kellett, ' None insists with more determination that morality is not mere convention, but something eternal.'[1] For Zoroaster, the proper study of mankind was God ; yet he did not attribute the province of God merely to the realm of spirit, removed from the practical matters of life. The Prophet would have men recognize two worlds, interpenetrating, and he himself prays for the blessings of both : ' I who would serve you, Mazdah Ahura and Good Thought—do ye give through the Right the blessings of both worlds, the bodily and that of Thought, which set the faithful in felicity ' (Ys. XXVIII, 2). Haurvatat and Ameretat (Welfare and Immortality) would be anticipated here on earth, as well as experienced in Heaven. Zoroaster was feeling for what was ultimately expressed in the Christian doctrine of an Eternal Life which begins now and is a guarantee of the future. For him, the attainment of this was in large measure consequent on man's obedience to the highest ethical standards known, though the Persians taught that man's salvation depended not merely on his own good deeds, but also upon the good deeds of those whom he left behind him. The sense of a corporate responsibility was very strong, even from the earliest days, and contributed greatly to the value of a moral ideal for all men.

The Prophet realized that as a man thought in his heart, so he was. This conception was foreign to the Avesta generally, though Zoroaster had put consider-

[1] *Short History of Religions*, p. 383.

able emphasis on this remarkable truth. Moulton claims it to have been perhaps the most outstanding contribution of spiritual insight made by the reformer : ' The deepest and truest revelation made or adapted by our Sage is the doctrine that a man's self (daena) determines his future destiny. The doctrine is the more impressive because of its tacit rejection of an inherited dogma which re-appears, largely improved upon, in the Later Avesta.'[1]   The dogma referred to is that of Fravashi, or spiritual counterpart, with which we shall deal in a subsequent chapter. But Zoroaster taught a doctrine of free will, and of individual responsibility for all actions. Thus his teaching was largely in positive commands. Man's duty was to attend the worship of Ahura and his good Spirits, to tend the sacred fires of the temples, and to avoid uncleanness, ceremonial and otherwise. But ritual observances were not to take the place of practical goodness. Thus hospitality and charity were placed high in the scale of virtues, as was also kindness to animals. Certain forms of sacrifice seem to have been tolerated, and there is no direct prohibition of images in the Gathas. The reformation had been sweeping, yet for the most part in vain ; once more a prophet had been too great for his people.

[1] *The Treasure of the Magi*, p. 36.

CHAPTER III

THE SCRIPTURES OF ZOROASTRIANISM

THE discovery of the key to the understanding of the Avesta, the Bible of the Parsis, is a romantic story. In the year 1754, a young Frenchman, Anquetil du Perron, saw a few pages of a manuscript in an unknown Oriental tongue, in a library at Paris. His interest and curiosity were so awakened that he determined at all costs to decipher the writing. He thereupon joined the French East India Company as a ranker, and embarked on a ship bound for Bombay, the centre of the Parsi community in India. After a hazardous journey, he reached his destination, and the French authorities honoured his purpose by releasing him from duty, and by granting him a certain amount of support. Although at first du Perron could find no one to teach him the language, eventually, through bribing an erudite priest, or Dastur, he acquired the requisite knowledge for his task, and also secured nearly two hundred manuscripts. The Parsis were very suspicious of the intruder, and he had to return to France to do his work of translation. This occupied du Perron ten years, but in the year 1771 he was able to publish a volume which he called *Zend-Avesta, Ouvrage de Zoroastre*. That this title was misleading will be shown later, but du Perron had rendered magnificent pioneer service to Iranian scholarship.

The reception given in Europe, however, to his work was by no means favourable, as the Persian scholars of the day, such as Sir William Jones, did not believe in a separate Avestan dialect, which was postulated by du Perron.

Although the discoverer was right in his assumption, the translation he then made cannot now be relied upon, as it contains many inaccuracies and reflects in parts his somewhat credulous disposition. Nevertheless, it was to be expected that du Perron's work would be inaccurate as the Parsis themselves knew the translation of their own Books only through the medium of a disused language, Pahlavi. The verbal traditions, however, that du Perron had received from his Parsi instructor were of great reliability. Many of the names of ancient Persian deities, hitherto unknown, were revealed, and most valuable light was thrown on old customs and ceremonial. But the authorities decried du Perron's work as a hoax, and naturally it was pointed out that the contents of the Avesta to a large extent did not accord with what was known of the teaching of Zoroaster. The lack of resemblance between the Avestan language and modern Persian was held to be sufficient reason for denying the genuineness of what du Perron had produced. Although du Perron's work gained some credence in France, the general opinion of European scholarship was hostile to it.

Some fifty years later, another Frenchman, Eugene Burnouf, who believed in the so-called Avestan tongue, carried out further research into the philology of the language, and corrected many of du Perron's obvious mistakes. Burnouf did valuable work on the grammatical side, but did little to sift the manuscripts

before him as to relative importance in matter
of date or doctrine. It was, moreover, not yet realized
that the Gathas were the only likely relics of the
writings of Zoroaster himself. But Burnouf had
made possible the work of many subsequent invest-
igators such as Bopp, the grammarian, Brockhaus, the
lexicographer, and Westergaard, who published a
monumental compendium of the Parsi religion and
literature. These and many others have presented
to us through their researches both in Sanskrit and
Pahlavi, a fairly reliable text of the Avesta. Perhaps
the most comprehensive translation yet undertaken,
however, is that by James Darmesteter and L. H.
Mills, in the *Sacred Books of the East*. But this
translation cannot be taken as final, as much has been
added to the knowledge of the language since the
work was undertaken. Of course, previous to the
discoveries of du Perron, Europe had not been without
Persian Books of great antiquity, but few could be
understood. The statements of Greek and Roman
writers concerning Zoroastrianism had been collated,
and Thomas Hyde, a famous Oxford scholar of the
early eighteenth century, had published a ' magnum
opus ' on the subject,[1] but it did not show much
knowledge of the original sources.

Although the expression Zend Avesta is widely
found, and was used originally by du Perron, it is
not an accurate description of the Bible of the Persians,
as the term means ' commentary on the Avesta.'
The derivation of the term ' Avesta ' is uncertain.
It is possibly akin to ' Veda,' i.e. Knowledge, ' vista '
being the past participle of the Sanskrit root ' vid,'

---

[1] Entitled *Historia Religionis veterum Persarum eorumque
Magorum*. Published A.D. 1700.

to know. More generally it is taken as coming from an ancient Avestan form 'upasta' which means 'the original text,' or 'scriptures.' Since Zend means 'commentary,' Avesta, simply, is the better title. As we now have it, the Avesta is only a fragment —though substantial at that—of a much greater literature, a great deal of which, some say two thirds, has been either lost or destroyed. A very small amount belongs to the period of the Prophet himself, though Pliny attributed to him two million verses. Zoroaster's output may well have been considerably greater than the Gathas : such an estimate as Pliny's, though of course absurd, affords, however, some indication of the immense labours of the followers of the Prophet.

The contents of the Avesta represent a long period of diverse development, and there are few religious Books in the world which present so many literary problems to the investigator. The original Avesta is said to have consisted of twenty one Nasks, or volumes, one for each word of the Ahuna Vairya formula (See ch. I). These were divided into three sections, each of seven groups, containing an encyclo-paedic account of Zoroastrian history, devotion and science. The 'science' was chiefly of an astronomical and astrological character. The Avesta was at first jealously guarded, and copies were preserved in the chief Fire Temples. The ravages of Alexander the Great (B.C. 330), however, were responsible for the loss and dislocation of a large number of Persian manuscripts, the nature of which can now be ascer-tained only through the evidence of those Books, such as the Dinkart, which contains summaries and quotations from the missing material. Diodorus the

historian records that when Alexander burnt
Persepolis, he put to death some of the leading scholars
who lived there, and their manuscripts perished with
them, as the Achaemenian stronghold was the repos-
itory of many Persian archives. The Arsacid king
Valkhash (c. second century B.C.)[1] was probably
the first to inaugurate a collation of the various
scattered manuscripts, and also caused many oral
traditions of Zoroastrianism to be committed to
writing. But it is doubtful whether the priests of
those times could compose in the same language as
the original Avesta. It was not until Sassanian days
(third and fourth centuries A.D.) that a comprehensive
collection of Books was made. The first Sassanian
monarch, Ardashir-i-Papakan, (226-240), by the help
of his high priest, Tansar, produced a text of the
Pahlavi writings. Shahpur I (A.D. 241-272) and
Shahpur II (A.D. 309-380) were instrumental in
gathering further texts from different parts of India
and the Roman Empire. Adarbad Maraspand, the
prime minister of Shahpur II, made an arrangement
of all the resultant discoveries, and a Canon of Scripture
was announced.

This Canon of Parsi scripture includes all that
survives in an extinct language, Avestan, which few
Oriental scholars can understand. In fact, very
few Parsis know it, and many of the Zoroastrian
priests of the present day are compelled to recite
their sacred Books in words utterly meaningless both
to them and to their listeners. The modern translations of the Avesta, accepted by the Parsis, are in
part most inaccurate, and certain stereotyped and

---

[1] It is not certain which of the three kings who bore this name
was responsible for the work.

traditional interpretations are now accepted without question. The later Pahlavi writings have, for instance, seriously changed the names of many of the old religious terms of Persia, and the Pahlavi translations of the Avesta do scant justice to the greatness of the finer passages, especially in the Gathas. One result has been that Darmesteter's translation of the Gathas, founded largely on the Pahlavi, is rendered practically useless, as the translator did not rely on the Gathic Avestan, the only true text. Incidentally, Darmesteter relegated the whole Avesta to the period of the Neo-Platonic literature, as he considered the religious allegories of the Gathas to resemble those of Philo. His argument was that, before the Greeks, there had been practically no philosophical development—a very hazardous hypothesis. Carnoy has aptly suggested that Darmesteter's mistake was due to his identifying ethical abstractions with philosophical concepts. That many of the writings are the product of activity in the Christian era will not be disputed, but the Gathas, Yashts and Vendidad are among the documents of far earlier origin. It is extremely difficult to assign dates to many parts of the Avesta, and sometimes the only reliable evidence that can be so used is internal. The style and metre of the contents are rough indication of the period to which they belong. Many of the texts, however, are corrupt. An exception to this is the text of the Gathas. The conclusion is that the Gathas were regarded as especially sacred, and have suffered little from editors. This strengthens our hypothesis that they represent the actual teaching of the great Prophet. In the later Books textual alterations abound, together with obvious blunders and intentional scribal glosses.

We have in the Avesta a library of Books which extends, like our own Bible, over a period of a thousand years. But revelation, in the Avesta, does not culminate at the end of the period as it does in our own Bible : generally speaking, the finest Avestan works are the earliest chronologically. The process of compilation of the Avesta was roughly as follows. The sayings of the Prophet and those who immediately followed him were the first to be recorded, and are found in a dialect called ' Gathic Avestan.' These records were then edited and elaborated by successive generations, who used practically the same language. In process of time there was necessitated a new explanation of the original sayings. This was supplied in a similar dialect, known to us as ' Younger Avestan,' and was called Zend. After another lapse of time, the old sayings and the commentary on them were looked upon as one, and equally sacred. But since the various forms of the Avestan language had become obsolete, another Zend was made on the extant scriptures, in Pahlavi, which was the ordinary tongue of Persia during the Sassanian era.

Finally, there was the Pazand, or re-exposition of the whole lot. When Zend is spoken of as a language to-day, Pahlavi is usually meant, because the Zend language, if ever it existed as a separate tongue, has dropped out of use. Originally the term Avesta was used only of the writings of the Prophet and those who were closely associated with the early propagation of the faith. Later on, a wider significance was adopted, to include the commentaries, and because of the increasing difficulty of sifting the wheat from the chaff, all the traditional writings became adorned with the same halo of sanctity. It was not generally known what was from Zoroaster and what was not, and there was no doctrine of degrees of inspiration. The ancient Greek and Roman writers, as well as the Persians themselves, ascribed a great deal that was obviously not Zoroaster's to his authorship. Just in the same way, Moses was long accredited with the account of his own death ! The difficulties involved in the theory that Zoroaster was responsible for the bulk of the Avesta were overcome by the assumption that the Nasks were dictated to the Prophet, as they stand, through divine revelation. Thus chronological obstacles were neatly swept away, as God could dictate words and phrases appropriate to a generation to come, and was not limited to the vocabulary or thought-forms of Zoroaster.

There is no statement in the earliest Persian Books as to who transcribed the narrative of the experiences or message of Zoroaster. Unlike Muhammad, the Prophet of Iran does not seem to have been commanded to publish the visions he had received. It is possible that Zoroaster himself wrote nothing, but that his friends and disciples transcribed his sayings ; parallels to this may be found in the composition of the Christian Gospels and the Vedic hymns. But there is an atmosphere of personal reminiscence in the Gathas which would suggest that the Prophet at least dictated some of the Yasnas. The oral tradition which is manifest in many portions of the Avesta is responsible for a certain amount of inaccuracy. Haug thinks that the majority of the Parsi scriptures were written down when their language was unintelligible to the scribes. Various additions to the manuscripts were made by the high priests in particular. In later days

4

it was believed that the high priests, who claimed
to be in the succession of Zoroaster, were given inspiration to interpret his mind without fail, and had
authority to add to his writings. This may partly
account for the tradition that Zoroaster was responsible for the whole of the Avesta.

The languages and dialects of the Avesta, which
have been outlined, are all inter-related. The Avestan,
in which the majority of the Books is written, is a very
rich tongue, making especially effective usage of
compound words which add colour and charm to the
narrative. It belongs to the Aryan family of languages,
and consequently has affinities with Greek, Latin,
Sanskrit and Teutonic forms. Of these, it is perhaps
closest to Sanskrit, as it is merely a different dialect
of the Sanskrit in which the Vedic books are found.
Haug maintains that the two dialects are as close as,
for example, the Ionic and Doric dialects of Greek :
' As the Ionians, Dorians, Aetolians, &c., were different tribes of the Greek nation, whose general name
was *Hellenes*, so the ancient Brahmans and Parsis
were two tribes of the nation which is called *Aryas*
both in the Veda and Zend-Avesta ; the former may
be compared with the Ionians, and the latter with the
Dorians . . . There can be no doubt that classical
Sanskrit was formed long after the separation of the
Iranians from the Hindus.'[1]

As to the relationship between the two main Avestan
dialects there is considerable dispute. It is difficult
even to prove that Pahlavi is less ancient than the
Gathic, as the latter may just have been a tongue
spoken in a different part of Iran. But grammatically,
the Gathic is more primitive, and the bulk of evidence

[1] *Essays on the Religion of the Parsis*, pp. 69-70.

favours its greater antiquity. Unfortunately, we have not much knowledge of the grammar of either dialect, and since the original forms of many words are now beyond recall, any translation is bound to be inadequate. Because of this, we have to pardon the great variations in the rendering of the Avesta, which are at times at least disconcerting. When the translations of Moulton, Darmesteter, Haug and Spiegel, for instance, are compared, it is sometimes quite a task to recognize the same passage so variously translated ! The available texts have, moreover, presented the greater difficulty to the translators in as much as many of the Parsis care little for the sense of the words in their scriptures, and are content if they are able to recite them.

In the Pahlavic sections of the Avesta, translation has been found easier, especially as there is a modern form of Pahlavi spoken to-day. The ancient form contained a number of Semitic words which had been incorporated during the period when Israel had close contacts with Persia ; to which period reference will be made later. Modern Pahlavi, however, has assimilated Arabic forms to the general exclusion of the Semitic. A great need is for modern Parsi scholars to produce a critical edition of their own scriptures ; too long have they relied on the researches of Europeans and Americans. It is reported that the Dasturs of Bombay are attempting this task, and it is to be hoped that their labours will bear quick fruition. Since the Great War, and the untimely death of James Hope Moulton, there has been very little work attempted in the realm of Iranian studies.

It now remains to describe and discuss briefly the contents of the extant Avesta, with some reference

to the so-called 'deutero-canonical' literature. The
Avesta proper contains the Yasna and Gathas, the
Yashts, the Visperad, the Vendidad and a number
of smaller Books and fragments. The Gathas are
the most important part of the Yasna. They have
been described as 'metrical sermons' and contain
most of what is known of the teaching of Zoroaster
himself. Their metre is not of a nature that lends
itself to translation in English verse, and it is unfortunate that the remoteness of many of the Gathic
allusions and the inadequacy of any rendering of them
have put these remarkable poems out of the reach
of the general reader, together with the rest of Persian
poetry. There has, alas, been only one Persian poem
which has made special appeal to the West—the
Rubáiyát of Omar Khayyám. But this was largely
due to the wonderful translation of Edward Fitz
Gerald. Says Moulton : ' Would Omar have been
heard of in English literary circles had (say) Carey
translated him ? '[1] But Omar comes from a period
very different from that which is our present concern,
for the date of the Gathas is something like three
thousand years ago. Considering this vast age, it
is more than remarkable that such fine literature,
nobler by far than the later Avesta, should find birth
in a primitive civilization. There is more colour and
movement in the language of the Gathas than in the
somewhat conventional phraseology of the subsequent
Books, and the strong personality of the Prophet
outstands through all these poems that tell the story
of his ministry. Although their language is obscure,
and the text mutilated, there remains, as Söderblom
remarks, ' a notable sureness of style. Comparison

[1] *Early Religious Poetry of Persia*, p. 2.

with the Veda hymns of the earlier period leads us to suppose that the art of verse was highly developed even in Indo-Iranian times before the eastward bound Aryans had been split between India and Iran. Zarathushtra or his friends were able to move in this heavy, artificial armour, so to speak, and these queer, twisted, complicated, and abstruse expressions. From these complicated verses and stanzas we can picture a very early and simple civilization, and a burning prophetic zeal.'[1] We need to remind ourselves that a simple civilization often may produce great poetry. Examples of this abound in the Old Testament, whilst Arab farmers and shepherds have shown no small poetic gifts.

The metre of the Gathas is very different from that of the later Avesta : Moulton likens it to that of *Hiawatha*, as it is also octosyllabic. One Gatha, however, is in prose. This is the Yasna haptanghaiti, or Seven Chapter Gatha, a collection of prayers addressed not only to Ahura, but to his surrounding Spirits (the Amesha Spentas) and the genii of the elements. In style and in doctrine this Gatha differs greatly from the others ; it is later, and represents the trend of the faith after the death of the Prophet. The old Nature deities which Zoroaster had banished, here return, though Ahura Mazdah is still supreme. A parallel process which may be observed in the early history of 'Christianity : some of the dethroned pagan gods returned as Christian saints, with scarcely a change of name. Later still, when Zoroastrianism came under Magian influence, yet more banished deities were restored.

In all, the Gathas are seventeen hymns, or poems,

[1] *The Living God*, pp. 187-8.

and their arrangement is according to their metres,
of which there are five. The first word in each
section determines their name. The Ahuna Vairya
formula, which has previously been referred to, is
also appended to the Gathas, together with a few
other passages especially suitable for repetition, such
as the Ashem Vohu, a proverbial saying to the effect
that Right rights itself.

The Yasna, of which the Gathas are a part, has
seventy two chapters, and is a liturgical compendium
meant to be used in connexion with the ceremonies
connected with the drinking of the Haoma plant.
There are three divisions in this Book : invocations,
hymns and commentary. Some of these hymns are
known as Yashts, and are dedicated to Angels. But
there is also a separate Book of Yashts, comprised
of twenty one poems of praise. Chief among the
Angels, or Yazatas, are Mithra, Anahita and Sraosha.
Some of these Yashts are very fine literature, but they
are most unequal in merit. It is likely that many
belong to the Achaemenian period, though they
incorporate and adapt earlier material for purposes
of worship under later conditions. The Visperad
is included in the Yasna, and is a series of disconnected
invocations to many deities—thus by derivation its
name means 'to all the lords.' It personifies many
of the heavenly bodies. The Vendidad means ' law
against the demons,' and is a late Book dating from
about the second century B.C. Many early legends
are recorded in this work, such as the story of Yima,
the Persian Noah. The story is also told of the
temptation of Zoroaster to worship the Daevas.
Three chapters are devoted to instructions as to the
way in which true Zoroastrians treat their dogs—as

dogs are regarded as sacred creatures among the Parsis. There is also a list given of things clean and unclean, as touching ceremonial, and methods of avoiding defilement are specified in detail. This strange Book is mainly cast in dialogue form, the Prophet asking questions and receiving answers of Ahura. The above works, with the addition of various small fragments, complete the contents of the Avesta proper.

The deutero-canonical literature is written in ' Middle Persian,' or Pahlavi, which was the language of Persia between about the third century B.C. and the ninth century A.D. These Pahlavi writings are an attempt to explain the Avesta which, together with the Zend, is attributed to Zoroaster himself. By this time the Prophet had become regarded as a supernatural being, and his teaching was neglected while his person was exalted. The Dinkart, composed about the ninth century A.D., is a summary and exposition of the Avestan texts and Zend known to the author, who by his quotations exhibits knowledge of a greater number of Avestan Books than we now possess. It is a huge volume of over a thousand pages, although the first two treatises are lost : among the remaining contents is a very fanciful life of the Prophet. The Bundahish and the Zartusht Namah are two later Books, written in Persian, subsequent to the invasion of Islam. The latter bears the date of A.D. 1277, yet purports to give accurate information of the details of the life of Zoroaster. The Bundahish, probably of somewhat earlier date than the Zartusht Namah, is a kind of ' Enquire within upon Everything ' concerning medieval Zoroastrianism. Among the host of less important Pahlavi Books, only two need here be mentioned—the Arda-Viraf and the Dadistan-i-Dinik. The former is an interesting sixth century account of the nature of Heaven and Hell, and the latter a series of questions put to a ninth-century priest, together with his answers. These deutero-canonical Books form what is known as the Kordah, or little, Avesta. Modern Persian translations of this Kordah Avesta have been published, and are of some use in determining the meaning of words that are obscure in the Pahlavi, but often they paraphrase rather than translate literally.

There are no manuscripts of the Avesta earlier than the thirteenth century A.D., the majority belong to the seventeenth. Not only did the old manuscripts suffer mutilation from Alexander the Great, for the Muhammadans also destroyed many Zoroastrian Books. The Quran was offered as a substitute for the Avesta, at the point of the sword. Although many faithful Zoroastrians refused to accept it, others acquiesced on the ground that many of the doctrines of the Avesta were also to be found in the Quran. A certain number of Persian religious ceremonies were allowed by the Moslem conquerors, and some of the old Fire Temples remained. But the glory of Persia had departed.

CHAPTER IV

DOCTRINE OF GOD

WE have so far assumed that Zoroaster was a monotheist. Such a supposition, however, is not without difficulties. Some have termed the Prophet a dualist, others a henotheist, others a kathenotheist ! In this chapter we shall give reasons for maintaining our conclusions. First, however, the name Zoroaster used for God must be considered. Ahura Mazdah, originally two dissociated words, was the name given, and signifies ' the wise lord.' Later, the name became known as Auramazda, or Ormuzd, in its Parsi form. Sometimes, the title Mazdah was used alone. The word Ahura is probably the same as the Aryan Asura, which may be identified with Varuna who is associated with Mitra in the Brahmanic Vedas. Both Ahura and Varuna are surrounded by a ' cabinet ' of ministering Spirits. Further links with Brahmanical cults will be brought to notice especially in this chapter.

Inasmuch as the primary test of any religion is in its doctrine of God, Zoroastrianism stands very high. Moulton used to tell his students that Zoroaster taught nothing about God which a Christian would not endorse, though there is much that a Christian should add. Such a statement is somewhat difficult to accept without reservations, and represents Moulton's own view that the Prophet was an uncompromising

monotheist. We feel, however, that although the
Prophet was by personal conviction a monotheist,
much of his teaching on, for example, the divine
Attributes and the reality of evil, leaves room for
other interpretations, as indeed there have been.
Perhaps Zoroaster himself did not foresee the implication of some of his doctrines, as ' a true prophet always
says more than he knows.' The evidence for determining Zoroaster's doctrine of God must be taken
from the Gathas alone, and from them must be
excluded the ' Seven Chapter Gatha ' of late origin
and manifestly polytheistic tendency.

The Avesta generally does not represent the Prophetic
teaching with faithfulness. As a background to
the Gathas, moreover, it must be remembered that
Zoroaster came to a people who worshipped a host
of Spirits called Ahuras. Zoroaster for good reason
did not change the name, but declared that Ahura
was one, and was all-wise : thus the name Mazdah,
again not new as a divine epithet. In the Gathas
this Ahura Mazdah is portrayed as One God whose
requirements are moral. Justice and truth must
be rendered as his service by men of good speech,
good thought and good deeds. His worshippers
must, in the power of Ahura, oppose all falsehood,
and apply themselves to the building up of society
in righteousness. Any unworthy conception of God
was evil : thus Zoroaster's strong insistence upon
truth as the opposite of evil. Ahura, in the Gathas,
is the creator and bestower of every good gift—' By
his holy Spirit and by Best Thought, deed, and word,
in accordance with Right, Mazdah Ahura with Dominion and Piety shall give us Welfare and Immortality '
(Ys. XLVII, 1). But in that Ahura created all

things, he was in measure responsible for the evil creation. Here difficulties arise, and the evidence must be examined carefully. A passage from one of the Yasnas is perhaps the best introduction—Ahura says, ' The more beneficent of my two Spirits has produced, by speaking it, the whole rightful creation, which is, and was, and will be, through the operation of the actions of life towards Mazdah.' These two Spirits are clearly Spenta Mainyu, the holy Spirit, and Angra Mainyu, the evil Spirit. Thus the evil Spirit is of Ahura. Although this passage is not from the Gathas, but from the nineteenth Yasna (v. 19), it is illustrative of their teaching of a God who ' at his will maketh us weal or woe ' (Ys. XLV, 9). In the same Gatha, the Prophet declares ' I will speak of the Spirits twain at the first beginning of the world, of whom the holier thus spake to the enemy : " Neither thought nor teachings nor wills nor beliefs nor words nor deeds nor selves nor souls of us twain agree " ' (Ys. XLV, 2).

In another Gatha we read ' Now the two primal Spirits, who revealed themselves in vision as Twins, are the Better and the Bad in thought and word and action. And between these two the wise once chose aright, the foolish not so. And when these twain Spirits came together in the beginning, they established Life and Not-Life, and that at the last the Worst Existence shall be to the followers of the Lie, but the Best Thought to him that follows Right. Of these twain Spirits he that followed the Lie chose the worst things ; the holiest Spirit chose Right, he that clothes him with the massy heavens as a garment ' (Ys. XXX, 3-5). Such passages as these are the backbone of the theory that Zoroaster was a dualist. But the claim cannot stand when it is remembered that the Prophet subordinates the two Spirits to Mazdah himself, who speaks of them as ' my Spirits.'

Moulton has well argued that the meaning of such Gathic passages is that the good Spirit of Ahura is not entirely free to do as he wills, as ever since he came into being there has been opposition from the evil Spirit : thus in a real sense the good and the evil are ' Twin Spirits.' A dualism of co-eternal Spirits is not taught in the Gathas ; they maintain that the evil Spirit will ultimately succumb to the good. Only once does the name of Ahriman, afterwards recognized as the Devil, appear in the Gathas. The Gathic teaching is that the enemies of Ahura Mazdah are the Daevas and the Lie (Druj), rather than Angra Mainyu or Ahriman. Later, however, the whole scheme of things was changed, and Spenta Mainyu was used as a name for Ahura himself. Thus Angra Mainyu, separated from God, became the Devil. We cannot claim that a doctrine of the Devil comes from the Prophet. Nevertheless, the present writer was interested to read recently in a book professing to give an outline of the religions of the world, that the importance of Zoroaster lay chiefly in the fact that ' he invented the Devil ' !

The Prophet was an optimist. Good would ultimately prevail : the evil Spirit is doomed to failure ere he begins his work. This was an essential part of the good news according to Zoroaster. But there seem to have been definite dualistic tendencies in the thought of the people to whom Zoroaster ministered. Had it not been for this, the Prophet might have been the founder of an entirely monotheistic system, with no loophole for dualism. In the Gathas we see, however, a doctrine of 'two worlds' of spirit and matter, which when misinterpreted, as was easily done, provided the basis of many strange doctrines that were afterwards foisted on the Prophet. Yet many Parsi scholars to-day still maintain that the faith of Iran has never been dualistic. E. W. West agrees with this, and Moulton holds that if we are to judge Parsism by the Prophet alone, there is no more dualism in it than there is in Christianity. Dr. Casartelli, the late Roman Catholic Bishop of Salford, who was Moulton's friend and co-investigator, has summed up the point at issue by showing that this question of dualism in Zoroastrianism is merely one of terms. We cannot, therefore, state with certainty whether this or that was meant by the compilers of the various Avestan Books until their vocabulary and style are examined individually. But the position of the Prophet, in the Gathas, is evident. Zoroaster recognized the existence and great power of evil in the world, from the beginning of all things, but was convinced that it could and would be overcome. Evil was continually to be fought, and prayer was to be offered for the victory of the good. In the meanwhile, Ahura would help those who helped him answer such petitions through their active resistance to all wickedness. Zoroaster himself never tried to placate evil, and never taught his followers to bow before it, as though its presence was a dread necessity. Self-control, rather than asceticism, was the means whereby it might be confronted.

In his desire to attribute all things to Ahura, Zoroaster had taken a dangerous step in postulating that the deity was limited by his own evil principle, and this position was denied by later writers. The

Prophet, however, had taught that though Ahura was good and beneficent, there existed in him the two primeval Spirits which are also in man, and between which a choice has to be made in every action. Moreover, it was sometimes the will of Ahura that evil should be sent for the discipline of men, that good might come of it. This thesis, found in the Gathas, is also shared by the Old Testament : it is the will of Jehovah to send a lying spirit into the mouths of four hundred prophets, says the compiler of the narrative of I Kings. In similar way, Amos declares that if the Assyrians descend on Israel, it is because Jehovah has sent them ; thus he writes, ' Shall evil befall a city, and the Lord hath not done it ? ' Isaiah also believes that although Jehovah is good, he will use the enemy as the rod of his anger, for all things are under his control.

Moulton's conclusion on the above problem in Zoroaster's own system is made with conviction—' I can see no evidence whatever to justify the imputation of dualism.'[1] At the same time, Zoroaster was very conscious of external forces in the world working for wickedness. But man, endowed with free will, could make choice, and refuse the evil : ' Bliss shall flee from them that despise righteousness. In such wise do ye destroy for yourselves the spiritual life ' (Ys. LIII, 6). Notice the emphasis on ' yourselves.' Again the note of personal choice is sounded in the verse ' Hear with your ears the best things ; look upon them with clear-seeing thought, for decision between the two Beliefs, each man for himself before the Great Consummation ' (Ys. XXX, 2). The insinuations of evil may be turned aside by the faithful :

[1] *Early Zoroastrianism*, p. 126.

'Let none of you listen to the liar's words and commands; he brings house and clan and district and land into misery and destruction. Resist them then with the weapon!' (Ys. XXXI, 18).

Zoroaster's concern with the problem of evil was mainly of a practical nature—how could man best fight wrong? The Prophet may or may not have believed in a personal Devil, but he did not theorize about him. For practical purposes he personified the enemy as the Druj, or Lie, who attacked man from within, and was the foe of Truth. The Daevas were, moreover, distinct from the 'Twin Spirits' of Ahura. Thus the famous Gathic passage: 'Between these two (Spirits) the Daevas also chose not aright, for infatuation came upon them as they took counsel together, so that they chose the worse thought. Then they rushed together to violence, that they might enfeeble the world of man' (Ys. XXX, 6). These Daevas, the relics of the old gods prior to the reform, are always considered evil by the Gathas, especially as they were the deities of the tribes who raided the Iranian farmsteads—'robber gangs, both Daevas and men' (Ys. XXIV, 5). They must be opposed by all good Zoroastrians: 'I declare myself a Mazdah worshipper, a Zoroastrian, an enemy of the Daevas, holding Ahura's law' are the words of the earliest known Zoroastrian creed.

It has been held that the Prophet was by philosophy a dualist, and by religious belief a monotheist. There is much to be said for this view, were it not for the fact that Zoroaster was no philosopher. He never purported to give a philosophical explanation of evil; his approach was entirely from the religious aspect. Nevertheless, even as all men have some philosophy of life not necessarily originating from religious convictions, Zoroaster also had his. A tendency to philosophic dualism is apparent on reading the Gathas, but all the while it is only a shadowy background. Zoroaster would interpret life and its problems from the standpoint of religious revelation rather than philosophic speculation. Moreover, to look for a logically consistent system at so early a period in the development of Eastern thought, is expecting too great things. To-day, there are eminent philosophers who feel that the antinomies of reason and revelation may best represent truth when left unreconciled. In his day, therefore, the Prophet taught a spiritual monotheism, behind which was a tendency to philosophic dualism based on moral grounds.

In the Gathas there is no mention of ' Zervan,' or Endless Time, a philosophical concept adopted by later Parsi writers in their attempt to explain the origin of the two conflicting principles within Ahura. Neither did Zoroaster hold the theory of the Gayomartians, a Zoroastrian sect, who maintained that the good Spirit himself was the Father of the Evil, which arose through a perversion of his mind. Ahura, taught the Prophet, created everything, though all things were not yet subject to his good Spirit. In such Avestan Books as the Vendidad we find a distinction between the creatures fashioned by Ahura, and those made by Ahriman. Long lists were given of the two kinds of creation : the Vendidad names the evil creatures and plagues which were believed to be the handiwork of Angra Mainyu, so too the Bundahish, where locusts, wolves, worms, snakes and other ' unclean ' animals made by the Evil One are contrasted with crows, dogs, foxes, and goats, which belonged to Ahura Mazdah's creation. Here, the Evil Spirit is a real creator, and therefore, says Casartelli, we may call this true dualism. Yet Angra Mainyu is all the while doomed, and thus a strange doctrine of semi-monotheism emerges, despite the fact of two creative powers; true dualism postulates that the two powers be co-eternal. Such divisions between the good and bad creation are foreign to the thought of Zoroaster, who had merely said that certain men or creatures, by act of choice, could put themselves on the side of the Druj. As the opponent of Asha (Truth), the Druj represented the falsehood of the old gods, and the name may possibly have been given by Zoroaster to a deity especially honoured under the pre-reformation régime. Schrader holds that the name had been used for malevolent ghosts. Later, in the Achaemenian age, the Druj became identified with Ahriman, the Devil. The emphasis Zoroaster placed on Truth as the chief requisite of Ahura was proudly retained by the Persians long after much else of the Prophetic teaching had been rejected or forgotten. In a notable account of the warlike Persians of his day, Herodotus remarked, ' They teach the boys, from five years old to twenty, three things only—to ride, to shoot, and to be truthful. . . . Most disgraceful of all is lying accounted.' Just as the Hebrew Psalmist declared, ' Behold, thou desirest truth in the inward parts,' Zoroaster knew that the God whose eye nothing escaped, hated falsehood outward and inward : ' Whatsoever open or secret things may be visited with judgement, or what man for a little sin demands the heaviest penalty—of all this through the Right thou art ware, observing them with flashing eye' (Ys. XXXI, 13).

5

One passage in the Gathas makes practical identification of Spenta Mainyu with Ahura Mazdah himself. Perhaps Zoroaster saw beyond the earlier conception that God has Spirit, and caught a glimpse of the higher revelation, that God is Spirit. Thus with vivid phrase, he declares, ' The holiest Spirit chose Right, he that clothes himself with the massy heavens as a garment ' (Ys. XXX, 5). The Prophet's idea of God is remarkably lofty : Ahura Mazdah is closely associated with the powers of Nature, as the above quotation indicates, yet is never identified with them. Ahura is above all natural forces, creating and controlling them. It is a false assumption that Zoroaster taught the worship of the sun, or any of the heavenly bodies, though this is frequently attributed to him. Zoroaster took fire as the *symbol* of the Divine, even as did another, who wrote ' Our God is a consuming fire.' Fire is a noble symbol of purity, and ' No Christian who remembers his own scriptures can cavil at such a symbolism as this.'[1] That Zoroaster's attitude on this matter should be later misinterpreted, was natural ; the sun became an object of worship. The Book of Ezekiel bears evidence of such practices, for they had penetrated even the Jewish Temple—' At the door of the temple of the Lord, between the porch and the altar, were about five and twenty men, with their backs toward the temple of the Lord, and their faces toward the east, and they worshipped the sun toward the east ' (VIII, 16). Or again, Herodotus records that the Persians ' sacrifice also to Sun, Moon, Earth, Fire, Water, and Winds. To these alone they have sacrificed from the beginning, but they have learned in addition, from

[1] Moulton, *The Teaching of Zarathrushtra*, p. 15.

the Assyrians and the Arabians, to sacrifice to Urania.'
Herodotus, however, knew little of the history of the
reform, and in describing Persian practices, relied
too greatly on contemporary tradition.   It is true
that there are Yashts in honour of the Sun and the
Moon, and that the 'Seven Chapter Gatha' tells of
worship of Earth and Water : the customs mentioned
by Herodotus must have been very ancient, but they
were not in accord with the teaching of the Prophet.

Zoroaster's doctrine of God avoided pantheism.
God and the universe are separate : Ahura is high
and lifted up above men.   But through the attributes
which are within Ahura's own Being, men can understand God's manifold activity in the world.   These
Attributes of Ahura, for which Zoroaster himself
seems to have given no collective name, were later
called the Amesha Spentas, or 'Glorious Immortal
Ones.'   In the Gathas constant mention is made of
them, as belonging to the essential nature of Ahura :
sometimes they seem identified with him, at other
times separate.   Later theology separated six of
these Amesha Spentas, regarding them as Archangels
or gods subordinate to Ahura.   Plutarch, writing
in the first century A.D., calls them 'six gods,' yet
this is untrue to the Prophetic doctrine.   Zoroaster
saw that a monotheism which conceived of God as an
undifferentiated unity would be incomprehensible—
'I believe Zarathushtra caught the great truth
which lies at the centre of the Christian doctrine
of the Trinity—that we cannot properly understand
the Unity of God without realizing a diversity within
His unity.   The pure white light of the sun is made
up of the colours of the rainbow.'[1]

[1] *Op. cit.*, p. 13.

Zoroaster did not speculate concerning the origin or nature of the Amesha Spentas, yet contrived to picture them as not detracting from the glory of Ahura. In fact, Ahura himself is sometimes reckoned among the Amesha Spentas, and has to be counted one of their number if, as Persian theology supposed, there were seven. On the other hand, Obedience (Sraosha) is sometimes introduced together with Destiny (Ashi) and the Ox-Soul (Geush-Urvan) as ' extra ' Attributes. That the conception of Amesha Spentas was new, is unlikely : Zoroaster probably moulded this ' cabinet ' around Ahura from the old gods, whose functions were all summed up in him. It is difficult to ascertain how far the Amesha Spentas were personified by the Prophet. Casartelli likened them to Bunyan's personifications of the good and evil elements in human character, yet the Amesha Spentas were hardly as ' concrete ' as Bunyan's figures, for they were essentially abstractions of God. Moulton has pointed out that, in the Gathas, the Amesha Spentas have gender, but no sex ; the first three are grammatically neuter, and the remaining three, which are grammatically feminine, are no more female than the others are male. These abstractions, believed to have emanated from Ahura himself, are eternal with him ; through them he guides and governs the world. No man has ever seen them, and their abode is in Paradise. Unlike Ahura, they are not infinite.

With the Amesha Spentas of Zoroaster we may compare the ' Dunameis ' of Philo, which also were intermediary between God and the world. Although most of Philo's ideas were either Greek or Jewish, there is strong Persian colouring to his thought.

Philo had horror of any anthropomorphic idea of God : God embraces everything, yet is embraced by nothing, He is the All. Thus, when God said, ' Let us make man,' Philo interpreted these words to the effect that Jehovah had called on the assisting heavenly beings to undertake the task for Him, and especially to undertake the less pleasant tasks of creation ! Such an idea is Platonic, as well as later Persian, for Plato's God leaves the evil work of the creation to the lesser members of the Pantheon.

The Logos, or creative instrument of God, according to Philo, was One with the Father. There were Logoi also, who were associated with the Angels of God, and several of these partake of the work of the Zoroastrian Amesha Spentas. Philo's Dunameis are more akin : they are not separated from God, but fill the world with His presence, and keep it in harmonious relationship. In one famous passage of Philo's *De Profugis* the Dunameis are, as sometimes in the Avesta, limited to six. They symbolize six cities of refuge. The Gathas nowhere use this simile for the Amesha Spentas, and the number may be mere coincidence. A few scholars, amongst them Darmesteter, have held that many Persian writings are indebted to Philo. This is unlikely. Dr. L. H. Mills's conclusion was the reverse : ' Philo drank in his Iranian lore from pages of his exilic Bible, or from the Bible books which were as yet detached, and which not only recorded Iranian edicts from Persian Kings, but were themselves half made up of Jewish-Persian history.'[1] Another parallel to the Amesha Spentas is to be found in the Adityas, the Vedic sun-gods of India. The god Asura is likewise surrounded by a host of

[1] *Zoroaster, Philo, the Achaemenids and Israel*, p. 206.

Adityas in a manner that closely resembles Ahura
with his Amesha Spentas : probably the two conceptions come from the same ancient Aryan belief.
In later Zoroastrian theology, there is yet another
' cabinet ' of Spirits ; gathered around Ahriman are
six archfiends, who oppose the work of the Amesha
Spentas.   The Vendidad names them—Akah Manah,
Indra, Sauru, Naonhaithya, Tauru, and Zairi.   Their
ultimate overthrow, however, is expected.

The Gathas attach epithets to the Amesha Spentas
which through constant use have become part of the
names themselves.   Thus, in the case of Vohu Manah,
the word ' Vohu ' is really an adjective meaning
' good.'   The other Attributes are Asha Vahista,
' Perfect Righteousness,' Khshathra Vairya, ' Wished-
for Kingdom,' Spenta Aramaiti, ' Holy Harmony '
or ' Devotion,' and Haurvatat and Ameretat (always
linked together), ' Salvation ' and ' Immortality.'
Vohu Manah, or ' Good Thought,' is a very beautiful
conception, being used both collectively and individually.   Moulton has summed the idea up by declaring
it to be no mere transcendental or philosophic virtue
practised by the ascetic, or holy-man, but is ' the
simple godliness of men and women living in the
world and doing their duty.'[1]   But Vohu Manah at
the same time is so much part of Ahura that sometimes when the Prophet addresses God he can say
' Thy Thought.'   The conception of Vohu Manah also
suggests Kindness as an Attribute of Ahura.   Thus
it is the requirement God makes of the heart of man,
both to his fellow creatures and to animals.
Zoroastrianism makes a strong protest against any
form of unkindness to animals, and especially those

[1] Moulton : *The Teaching of Zarathushtra*, p. 16.

that are useful in the home or on the farm. Appropriately, Vohu Manah was also a term used for Paradise. Originally, Vohu Manah was probably just the principle of beneficence attributed to Ahura and other gods, but the Prophet both enlarged and restricted its connotation.

Asha Vahista, or Perfect Righteousness, has wider meaning than the English suggests. In fact, translation by any single word is in most cases inadequate, when considering the Amesha Spentas. Asha is the rational Order and Design permeating the creation, which is therefore a universe, and not multiverse or chaos. Plutarch translated Asha by 'Truth,' and the meaning of the latter in the Avesta is sufficiently broad to admit this rendering, though it is not the best translation. The conception of Asha ensures the fact that the Law of the universe is part of the Being of God, and that the limitations this Law entails, are self-limitations on the part of the creator. This rational Order in the mind of God implied, according to Zoroaster, that He required sound judgement to be found of man ; justice and social equilibrium were to be its chief expression. Any breach of Truth was denial of Asha : Moulton holds that Zoroaster was the first to state that the Spirit of Truth was of the very nature of God. In so far as Asha denoted the established order of things as reflecting the Right Order in the mind of the creator, it also became associated with Piety, for which it is sometimes a synonym. In the Gathas, Asha is the first of the Amesha Spentas, though the later Avesta places Vohu Manah before it. Generally speaking, Asha is not personified to such an extent as is Vohu Manah, which is the most personified of all the Ameshas. The idea of Asha was an ancient Aryan legacy, and may be compared with that of Rita in the Vedas ; the root from which Asha comes is found in the many Persian names that begin with ' Arta,' e.g. Artaxerxes, &c. Asha also represented light and flame, partly because of their purity and partly because God's presence penetrates everywhere even as light does. The importance of Asha for Zoroaster's teaching about God can hardly be overestimated.

We now come to the Prophet's doctrine of God's kingdom, which he called Khshathra Vairya. As in the New Testament, it is both present and future, and its significance is eschatological in the main. Thus the association Khshathra has with metals is explained by Williams Jackson on the basis of the Persian tradition that the earth would finally be cleansed by a stream of molten iron. This seems strange when we remember that Khshathra was ' Vairya,' that is, ' Wished-for ' ; but it should be mentioned that the tradition adds that although the unrighteous would be consumed by this flood, the righteous would bathe in it as in warm milk ! In spite of these strange associations borne by Khshathra, it embodies not a few of the ideals of the Christian Gospel. ' The constant thought of the Kingdom of God as the supreme object of man's ambition is in the Gathas largely obscured for us by the difficult language ; but it is central, and there is no more significant link between the religion of the Iranian prophet and that of the Gospels.'[1]

Next of the Amesha Spentas is Spenta Aramaiti, ' Holy Harmony ' or ' Devotion,' who is called the daughter of Ahura Mazdah. Aramaiti signifies the

[1] Moulton : *Early Zoroastrianism*, p. 294.

God-given bond of union between the worshipper and the Deity. Once again was it emphasized that Ahura required devotion of a practical nature, not necessarily to be expressed in asceticism. Söderblom calls Aramaiti 'the Genius of pious resignation,' representing an obedient and devoted attitude to Ahura. Such a description, however, scarcely does justice to the constant activity for good that Zoroaster urged; devotion to Ahura was to be founded in a 'love of the brethren.' The name Aramaiti occurs in the Brahmanic Rigveda, meaning 'Earth,' but Aramaiti personified represents a maiden who brings daily offerings to the god Agni. Aramaiti as a term for the Earth is found in the Gathas. The Yasna XXX, 7, says that 'Aramaiti gave continued life to men's bodies, and indestructibility.' That is, Earth is so pure that she can cleanse the impurity of death. It seems that Zoroaster himself would not have approved of the later Parsi practice of giving the bones of the dead to the vultures, lest the ground should be defiled : there is no record that the Prophet or his near disciples underwent a 'burial' of this kind. Zoroaster seems to have taught that Aramaiti could overcome any ceremonial or natural contamination.

Haurvatat and Ameretat, 'Salvation' and 'Immortality,' are the last of the Amesha Spentas usually included in the 'cabinet' of Ahura. Haurvatat is sometimes translated 'Spirit of Healthful Wellbeing,' and Ameretat 'Endless Existence.' Söderblom renders Ameretat as 'Ambrosia.' This pair of Attributes stand for the Salvation Ahura offers in this world and in the life to come : it is a fine thought that the two are not separated. In their earthly function,

Haurvatat and Ameretat take especial care of vegetation ; ' they represent the preservation of the original uncorrupted state of the good creation, and its remaining in the same condition as that in which it was created by God.'[1] Such, therefore, are the Spirits that surround the throne of Ahura, and partake of his unity.

Later, we find a very different story. Henotheism, and even polytheism, developed. The great Darius, professedly a monotheist, called Ahura only ' Greatest of Gods ' and associated others with him. Herodotus, who in his account of Zoroastrianism does not even mention the name of Ahura Mazdah, records that the Persians worshipped a sky-god, and yearly buried alive a number of noble youths and maidens as an offering to the god who lived under the earth. A number of ancient Aryan and Indian gods appear in the Avesta, and the teaching of Zoroaster is forgotten. Occasionally, however, the Vedic deities are the Avestan demons : such is Indra, mentioned in the Vendidad, the god in whose honour the Indians drank the intoxicating Soma, or as the Persians called it, Haoma. Other Vedic deities are the Angels of the Avesta ; amongst these is Mitra, a member of the Indian trinity. In one of the later Yashts, we find a Spirit named Vayu, who is mentioned in the Gathas (Ys. LIII, 6). Vayu is also in the Vedas, as one who ' first drinks the Soma at the morning sacrifice.' Haug somewhat ingeniously pointed out that there are thirty three Devas, or gods, recognized in the Vedas, which corresponds exactly with the number of Ratus, or Judges, enumerated in the first Yasna of the Avesta as instructed by Ahura Mazdah to

[1] Haug : *Essays on the Religion of the Parsis*, p. 307.

defend the Zoroastrian faith. The fact that there were thirty three in each case seems again to point to the common stock from which the two cults derived their conception of God.

From the time of Darius onwards, the Druj of the Gathas acquired the name of Ahriman. In the famous Behistun inscription, the two words ' Angra ' and ' Mainyu ' are combined, and practical identification between Angra Mainyu and Ahriman, the Devil, was made : later, the Magi were especially responsible for popularizing this usage. It was believed that Ahriman with his Angels arose out of the dark Abyss and attacked the Good Spirit, eager to destroy the Angels of Light. Ahriman, however, was repulsed by the power of prayer, and temporarily restrained. A long period follows during which neither Good nor Evil is victorious ; thus the present state of the world, with its abundant evidence of the existence of both right and wrong. This conflict, it was taught, is continuous, and all deeds done by those on earth helped one side or the other to victory. Such doctrine did well to maintain that man's resistance to evil in this life had eternal significance. The final stage would be the defeat of Ahriman and his Angels. Casartelli sums up this strange situation : ' We thus have a monotheism limited and modified by dualism, as well as a dualism modified by an ultimate monotheism.'[1] The entire system of the later Avesta is built around this doctrine of conflict between two opposing powers, of which the Evil Spirit has quite independent origin. There were, in fact, two creations, extending even among the heavenly bodies ; the

[1] Hastings : *Encyclopaedia of Religion and Ethics*, Vol. V, p. III.

stars belonged to the good, and the planets to the evil. This is indeed dualism, though a modern Parsi theologian, Rastamji Edulgi, has recently written in endeavour to prove that Spenta Mainyu and Angra Mainyu were not divine Spirits, but merely conflicting principles within men. This view, however, is not shared by the majority of Parsis.

In the Sassanian era the Pahlavi literature designates Ahura Mazdah or Ormuzd, as the name was then known, as intangible Spirit, who has initial advantage over Ahriman in that he can foresee the future and the day of his victory. Ahriman, however, can have knowledge only of the past, as he dwells in the realm of darkness, where there is no enlightenment. The dualistic thought of the Parsis could not admit the infinity of Ormuzd, and consequently it was allowed that Ahriman was really a limitation of him.

The name of Anahita was coupled in the later Avesta with Ahura and Mithra, completing a triad, similar to the Vedic Varuna, Mitra and Aryaman. In Strabo's account of the Persians, there is record of worship paid to Aphrodite, which was the name given by the Greeks to Anahita—' They (the Persians) honour also the Sun, whom they call Mithras, and the Moon, and Aphrodite, and Fire and Earth, and Winds and Water.' Whilst the Greeks, as we have just seen, sometimes identified Anahita with Aphrodite, the goddess of fertility, they also associated her with Athene, goddess of war. Some Persian branches of her cult, moreover, equated Anahita with the planet Venus, perhaps to make propitious this planet which was usually regarded as hostile to man. Anahita, or in full, Ardvi Sura Anahita, ' The High Powerful Immaculate One ' has an entire Yasht in her honour.

It is very doubtful, however, whether the worship of this goddess was indigenous to Persia. Possibly her cult was imported from the Elamites, or from some other people of Western Asia. Herodotus says it came from the Assyrians and the Arabians; but he makes an obvious mistake in stating that the Persians call Aphrodite Mithra. The Achaemenian inscriptions nevertheless closely link Anahita with Mithra, and sometimes a bull was slain in her honour, as in the rite of the Mithraic Taurobolium. In the inscriptions of Artaxerxes II we find prayers addressed to Ahura Mazdah, Anahita and Mithra alike. Artaxerxes also erected statues in honour of Anahita, representing her as a beautiful young woman with a golden cloak, sandals fastened with gold, a thousand gemmed coronet on her head, and holding in her hand a bunch of the sacred ' Baresman ' twigs. This accords roughly with the description given in the Aban Yasht which pictures Ahura Mazdah himself worshipping Anahita and offering to her libations in order that Zoroaster might be led into the paths of virtue and the true religion. The Yasht records that ' Anahita bestowed on him this blessing, even on him as he at once brought libations.' The worship of Anahita became very widespread : Pliny gives evidence that her cult extended to Armenia, whilst Strabo tells of its spread to Pontus, Cappadocia and Cilicia. Many inscriptions belonging to this cult have been found in Lydia. Anahita was worshipped there in Persian fashion, as the goddess of streams, having practically the same functions as the Chaldaic Ishtar and the Sumerian Nin-Ella.

In all this we see how far Parsism had gone from the

teaching of Zoroaster. Although the supremacy of
Ahura Mazdah remained technically, actually subordinate Spirits became more important, and these
Spirits now were not merely the Amesha Spentas, but
included the Yazatas or Angels, and the Fravashis.
(See next chapter.) The unresolved teaching in
the Gathas, with its allowance of evil Spirits, lent
itself to a dualistic interpretation among the mass
of the people. Zoroaster had given no really satisfactory explanation of the problem of the existence
of evil, he had merely postulated a kind of ' diabolus
ex machina,' though his followers simplified the
solution at least to their own satisfaction. The
Greek writers on Zoroastrianism in their day thought
that the late dualistic system was fathered by the
Prophet. But Zoroaster would rightly have disowned
such a child.

CHAPTER V

DOCTRINE OF MAN

It is intended in this chapter to give some account of the Zoroastrian doctrine of creation, of man's personality, and of his final destiny. But before considering the origin and end of man, it will perhaps be best to examine the teaching concerning his own self. Psychological doctrines of the nature of man are, of course, not developed in the Avesta which contains, however, a good deal of latent psychology. We do not find the usual tripartite division of man's personality into reason, feeling and will. Yet there is strong distinction made between the parts that were considered to be spiritual and those that were designated as physical. Especially should the insistent emphasis on the freedom of the human will be noticed. That man is free of will and morally responsible for his actions is axiomatic in Persian teaching. In collating the relevant passages we find that the human personality was conceived of as possessing five elements. These are—Vitality ('Ahu'), Ego ('Daena'), Perception ('Baodha'), Soul ('Urvan'), and Fravashi, the translation of which will be considered later.

The Ahu may be paralleled by the modern conception of Life-Urge or 'élan vital,' and shares many of the functions of the Baodha. In the Gathas, Ahu is very difficult to translate, but there seems to be distinction made between an Ahu bodily and mental,

or perhaps, spiritual. Dr. Geiger thinks, however,
that the existence of Ahu is determined by the co-
existence of the body, and that its function is to
preserve the life of man, as well as to strengthen his
moral apprehension. The Daena, or Ego, is that which
determines the destiny of man. Some translate it as
Conscience, for it includes man's individual sense of
responsibility. The doctrine of Daena was taught by
Zoroaster himself, who in the Gathas ignores the
popular conception of Fravashi, probably because of
its threat to monotheism as being a relic of ancestor-
worship. The existence of the Daena, which is
distinguished from the Urvan or Soul, is independent
of the body; some hold that it is eternal, acting as
a guide over the destiny of man before his birth,
during his life, and after his death. When a man
passes over to the other world, his Daena awaits him,
not his Fravashi, for a Fravashi can only be good.
If the Daena is good, then the righteous man travels
' the road of Good Thought, built by Right, on which
the Selves of the Future Deliverers shall go to the
reward ' (Ys. XXXIV, 13). The Daena takes the
form of a very beautiful maiden, or an ugly fiend,
according to the character of the life the man has
lived on earth. Moulton's verse translation of the
twenty-second Yasht gives a beautiful picture of a
noble Daena awaiting a man to guide him over the
Bridge of Judgement.

> ' Four glorious Dawns had risen,
> And with the wakening loveliness of day
> Came breezes whispering from the southern sky,
> Laden with fragrant sweetness. I beheld,
> And floating lightly on the enamoured winds
> A Presence sped and hovered over me,
> A maiden, roseate as the blush of morn,
> Stately and pure as heaven, and on her face

The freshness of a bloom untouched of Time.
Amazed I cried, " Who art thou, Maiden fair,
Fairer than aught on earth these eyes have seen ? "
And she in answer spake, " I am Thyself,
Thy thoughts, thy words, thy actions, glorified
By every conquest over base desire,
By every offering of a holy prayer
To the Wise Lord in Heaven, every deed
Of kindly help done to the good and pure.
By these I come thus lovely, come to guide
Thy steps to the dread Bridge where waits for thee
The Prophet, charged with judgement." [1]

Again we note the insistence that a man can make
or mar his own life and destiny—' Whoso, O Mazdah,
makes his thought now better, now worse, and likewise his Self (Daena) by action and by word, and
follows his own inclinations, wishes and choices, he
shall in thy purpose be in a separate place at the last '
(Ys. XLVIII, 4). Daena, in the Gathas, can signify
' Religious Law ' as well as the Self, and is used in
one passage in the sense of ' The Religion which is
the best for all ' (Ys. XLIV, 10).

Baodha, meaning Perception or Intelligence, is that
which illumines the body so that intelligence and
understanding may characterize the actions of man.
The Dinkart says, ' As the sun is the light of the
world, and a lamp is (the light) of a house, so does
the intellect (Bod, the Pahlavi form of Baodha)
animate with watchful light the lord of the house,
and so does it animate the rider on the horse, as also
it directs the master of the house to take care of the
house, and the rider of the horse ' (Dk. VI, 354).
Urvan, the Soul, is the possession not merely of men,
but of animals also, and is the true unity of the life
principle. Though quite independent of this world,
the Urvan may be effected by man's deeds, and it

[1] *Early Religious Poetry of Persia*, pp. 159-160.

6

is possible for the Soul to be 'lost.' Body and Soul
may be thrown into Hell if a man's mode of life has
been thoroughly wicked, but normally the Soul has
existence after the destruction of the body, with
which during life it has an integral relationship. The
Soul is best tended by good works done whilst a man
is still in the body. The Parsis believed that the Urvan
joined with the Fravashi at death, and they consequently worshipped it : 'We adore the sunny
abodes of Asha, wherein the souls (Urvan) of the dead
rest, which are the Fravashis of the righteous ' (Ys.
XVI, 7).

The Fravashi is the last of the component elements
in the personality of man summed up in the thirteenth
Yasht—' We adore the vitality, the self, the perception,
the soul, and the Fravashi of righteous men and
women who understand the Religion, who in present,
future, or past win the victory, who have won the
victory for Asha,' (verse 155). The word Fravashi
is, as we have noted, especially difficult to translate,
since it covers several meanings. Literally, the word
signifies 'Confession' or 'Conscience,' but Carnoy
holds that the origin of the term is to be found in
ancestor worship, and in the conception of household
gods ('di manes'), for the festival the Parsis keep
in honour of the Fravashis has all the character of
an 'All Souls' Day.' Another derivation of the word
Fravashi comes from a root meaning ' to impregnate ' ;
this suggests the reason why the Fravashis were
considered to be especially the Guardian Spirits over
birth. They kept watch over every man from the
day of his entry into the world, and are really the
prototypes of all life, both of man and of beast,
existing even before creation. The ox has a Fravashi,

the Geush-Urvan, which is the protector of all animals. It is difficult to make distinction between the conceptions of Fravashi and Urvan, but they are thought of as separate by the Parsis. The Prophet himself did not make use of the idea of Fravashi, partly because of its original non-ethical character and partly, as suggested, because it would have endangered his monotheistic doctrine by reason of pagan associations.

There are several parallel conceptions to that of Fravashi amongst other peoples than the Iranian. Dr. Dhalla likens the Fravashis to the 'Ideas' of Plato. The Roman idea of presiding 'Genii' who have special functions over matters of birth and death, and the Egyptian 'Ka' are not dissimilar. The Indian 'Pitaras,' like the Fravashis and the Roman 'Manes' depend on the correct performance of ritual on the part of their former relatives and friends. Also the Brahmanic conception of 'Atman' or Soul is parallel, except for the fact that all creatures whether good or bad possess Atman, whilst in the Avesta there is no reference to the Fravashi of a bad man or of any member of the evil creation. Some of the later Persian documents, however, say that the Fravashi of an unbeliever goes to Hell with him, but the earlier writings do not even record the possibility that an unbeliever should have a Fravashi. That Fravashis had separate function over the individuals they protected is doubtful, yet every child coming into the world was not without a Fravashi. Generally the Fravashis acted as a kind of 'guardian body' over, for example, agriculture and childbirth; in this latter respect their office overlapped with that of the goddess Anahita. The

Fravashis of departed saints were frequently worshipped, according to their specific abilities to drive
away demons, to bring success, or to heal diseases.
Nevertheless, departure from such association with
ancestor worship is noticeable in the fact that adoration was also given to the Fravashis of great men
yet unborn : the thirteenth Yasht, however, declares
that the strongest Fravashis are those of the living
faithful. This Yasht also enumerates the various
stars and forces of Nature which are made and con-
trolled by the Fravashis. Yet more frequently the
Fravashis were regarded as part of the human
personality, whilst at other times they are heavenly
Spirits. There were also Fravashis of clans and
households, as well as of individuals.

In the Pahlavic period we find many references to
Farohars, or Fravahars, which correspond to the
Avestan Fravashis, yet the doctrine concerning them
was not so spiritual, as the Farohars were the possession
only of those on earth. The Avesta taught that the
Heavenly Beings, including the Amesha Spentas, all
had their Fravashis. In later days, the whole
conception of Fravashi sadly degenerated : says Buch,
' in the post-Sassanian writings, it (*i.e.* the Fravashi)
becomes a mere principle of digestion '[1] giving whole-
someness to food. The Magians especially associated
the Fravashis with the heavenly bodies, as much of
their lore was on an astronomical basis. Herein,
Moulton suggests, may be the explanation of the story
told in the Gospel of St. Matthew (Ch. II) of the Magi
journeying from afar to worship the child Jesus.
A star of unusual brightness, newly appearing, might
have spoken to them of the Fravashi of some great

[1] *Zoroastrian Ethics*, p. 44.

man to be born. Also, the reference to the ' Angels of the Churches ' in the Book of Revelation, and to the ' Princes ' of the nations in Daniel and the Talmud answer in the main to the Avestan conceptions. There are, moreover, two New Testament passages of exceptional interest in this connexion, in that they speak in Persian fashion of Angels as the counterpart of those on earth. We cannot, of course, affirm that either of these references necessitates Zoroastrian influence, but the parallel is extremely suggestive. St. Matthew XVIII, 10, reads, ' Take heed that ye despise not one of these little ones ; for I say unto you that in heaven their angels do always behold the face of my Father which is in heaven.' By this may be meant the heavenly counterparts of those who are yet without sin. The Acts XII, 12-15, tells how the maid at the house of Mary at Jerusalem said that Peter was at the door ; those within denied that it could be he, but declared ' It is his angel,' or Fravashi.

The Persians conceived of the Fravashis both as representative and guardian Spirits. In a sense, they were the ghosts of the dead, but they held no terrors, as all Fravashis belonged to Ahura's good creation. The Avesta generally does not try to picture the various forms the Fravashis assumed ; an exception to this, however, is made by the thirteenth Yasht, which describes a Fravashi as ' flying like a well-winged bird.' With such a conception may be compared the Greek idea that the soul left the body in the shape of a bird. All living beings, including Ahura Mazdah himself, possessed Fravashis, and any or all of these might be the proper object of adoration by the good Zoroastrian. ' We adore the Fravashis

of the followers of Ahura, both men and women,'
says the Seven Chapter Gatha, which is the first to
make mention of Fravashis (Ys. XXXVII, 3). The
above quoted Yasht, which incidentally is the longest
Yasht in the collection, gives worship to a host of
Fravashis of famous saints and warriors who had
distinguished themselves during their lifetime.
Amongst these is Vishtaspa ' the attacker of demons,
the believer in Ahura ' (verse 99). The Fravashi of
Zoroaster also is to be adored—' We worship the
rule and the Fravashi of Zarathushtra Spitama, who
first thought good thoughts, who first spake good
words, who first performed good actions, who was
the first priest, the first warrior, the first cultivator
of the soil, the first prophet, the first who was inspired '
(verse 88). It was believed that if the Fravashis
of the righteous did not receive due attention, Ahriman
would be given power over the good creation as well
as over the evil. So zealous were the Fravashis for
the interests of the peoples they represented, that the
Yasht pictures a drought threatening the land and a
crowd of Fravashis rushing to a great lake called
Vourukasha, to secure water for the communities over
which they presided : so anxious were they to serve
their own folk that the Fravashis quarrelled among
themselves as to the appropriate supplies. The
Bundahish records that in the beginning the Fravashis
were given the option of remaining for ever in the
' heavenlies ' or of coming to earth to take part in
the eternal conflict waged by man against the forces
of evil. They chose the latter, and joined in the struggle
against Ahriman.

Since the human soul was believed not to leave the
body until four days after death, there were special

services offered to the Fravashi also on the fourth day. At the funeral ceremony, or 'Afringan,' food was offered for the use of the dead man and his Fravashi in the next world. The gardens that surround the Towers of Silence that are the burial places of modern Parsis are visited by friends of the dead, who on appointed days pay reverence to the Fravashis of the righteous, and make confession of their own sins. The specially appointed Pahlavi time for the worship of the Fravashis was the Hamaspathmaedaya, the New Year, corresponding to the middle of March in our own calendar, and the first month of the Persian year was named Fravardin in honour of the Fravashis. The nineteenth day of each month was also dedicated to them.

We now pass on to the Zoroastrian doctrine of creation, and of the origin of human life. As in other faiths, there was no realization of the long ages of cosmic development which preceded the entry of man, as he now is, into the world, though there was a doctrine of a spiritual world preceding the material. The older Avestan texts are not much concerned with theories of the origin of the world ; the Pahlavi literature, however, supplies full account in such Books as the Bundahish. The agent of creation is Ahura (Ormuzd) though sometimes the Amesha Spentas are mentioned as sharing his task : the Amesha Spentas are also represented as dwelling in the presence of Ahura in the ages previous to the creation. It is a matter of dispute whether creation ' ex nihilo ' was taught, though the Bundahish says that Ahura did not form the future out of the past. The original creation was entirely spiritual and intangible for three thousand years, which comprised

the first of the four 'world-periods' each of the same
duration. Angra Mainyu, the Devil, had lived apart
from Ahura Mazdah from countless time and had been
unaware of him, but when he saw light which Ahura
had made he attacked him, and set to work to overthrow the new creation by forming demons and evil
powers of all kinds. Thus a nine thousand years war
was begun. But in the first three thousand years of
this conflict, which was the second world-period,
Ahriman found that Ahura had means to counteract
his every design, and realizing that he had been
outwitted, Ahriman cast himself into a great abyss.

In the next period, however, Ahriman reappeared,
and viewing what Ahura had done, successfully
contrived himself to create all kinds of evil things,
including, says the Bundahish, 99,999 diseases. The
primal Man, Gaya Maretan, who had been created
along with the rest of the present creation during the
period when Ahriman had no power, was now slain
by Ahriman, together with the primal Ox. The final
stage in this conflict, nevertheless, is one of triumph
for Ahura, who drives the evil forces back to Hell.
A Deliverer appears, and heralds the beginning of a
new age. After each thousand years in this last period,
moreover, a new Deliverer is born of the line of
Zoroaster, who strikes another vital blow at Ahriman.
At the end of all, it was taught, Ahriman would
fall back once more into the abyss and mankind
would ascend to the realms of light to live for ever
with Ahura Mazdah. An account of the above tradition
is recorded by Plutarch, who received his information
from Theopompus (fourth century B.C.). 'According
to the Magi,' says Plutarch, 'one of the gods conquers
and the other is conquered for three thousand years

each; and for another three thousand years they fight and war, and one destroys the works of the other, but finally Hades loses, and mankind shall be blessed, neither needing nourishment nor casting shadows.'[1]

There are many curious stories told by the Pahlavi Books concerning the struggles of the two creations and their makers. One is that Ahura had set up a tree of life which would sustain all other trees and plants. In order to destroy this tree, Ahriman sent a great lizard of monstrous form, which arose from the lake Vourukasha. But the lizard was frustrated from its evil purpose by the Kar-fish Ahura had placed in the lake. In most of these stories, whenever Ahriman devises some clever plan Ahura forms a scheme still cleverer.

The first man, says the Pahlavi tradition, was born of the sweat of the creator, and was slain by Ahriman. On his death, his seed which had been miraculously preserved produced the first human pair, Mashya and Mashyoi, from whom originated the whole human race. The Vendidad tells of an earlier prophet than Zoroaster, Yima, to whom Ahura revealed himself. Although Yima was not able to proclaim to men the truth he had received, Ahura made him the protector of all creation. Under his care the creation multiplied to such an extent that the earth had to be enlarged thrice to accommodate it. After nine hundred years Ahura announced to Yima the approach of an ice age, during which the whole creation was to be destroyed, except two of each kind which Yima was to shelter, plant and animal life alike. Long after the death of Yima, however, Zoroaster himself received

[1] *De Iside et Osiride*, Ch. XLVII.

the full revelation which Ahura had been waiting to give to men.

This story of Yima is closely paralleled in the Brahman Rigveda, as well as in the Bible, for according to the Indian tradition, the first-born of men was named Yama, who was also the first of men to taste death. On finding that the future life was one of happiness, Yama returned to tell others that they had nothing to fear in death, for there awaited them a realm of bliss which nothing could take away. This latter belief corresponds with the Parsi teaching that Yima was to be the ruler of the Golden Age which was promised to the faithful. In the later Indian legends, however, Yama became a malevolent deity who presided over the functions of the wicked. Haug suggests the reason for this was because it was imagined that Yama had not been rightly propitiated : not infrequently in the East a god whose purpose was once beneficent is turned into an evil being. But in Zoroastrian thought, Yima was always the advocate of men.

Concerning the Zoroastrian doctrine of the origin of evil in the world, there is much dispute. A difficult passage in the Gathas has had many interpretations : ' To these sinners belonged, 'tis said, Yima also, son of Vivahant, who, desiring to satisfy mortals, gave our people portions of beef to eat ' (Ys. XXXII, 8). Moulton thinks that Yima here stands for Gaya Maretan, the first man, according to ancient Aryan folk-lore, and that he gave to men forbidden food which would make them immortal before their due time. Yima had been tempted by the Daevas to snatch Ahura's good gift before he was ready to give it, and before man could accept it, and thus they

' defrauded men of good life and immortality.' This forbidden food was probably the carcase of the primeval Cow from which, says the ancient Aryan tradition, man was created. Yima's own punishment, according to the Vendidad, was the loss of his ' Kingly Glory.' The world, instead of being a Paradise, became a battlefield of conflict between good and evil. One tradition pictures the world as divided into seven zones, a feature which in common with several other legends of cosmogony, may have been borrowed from Semitic thought. In each of these zones there is a battle between heat and cold, light and darkness, fertility and barrenness, destructive creatures and domestic animals, disease and health. Into this conflict man must enter : he is on one side or the other according to the quality of life which he lives.

Once again, despite the fantastic nature of some of the creation stories, we see how the problem of the presence of evil in the world was faced by Zoroastrianism in a thoroughly practical way. The Parsi was concerned with evil as an ethical dilemma to be lived out, rather than as a philosophical problem to be thought out and solved by reason. This attitude provides great contrast with the speculative and philosophic attitude of the Vedas. G. F. Moore has suggested that geographical influences may in part account for this : the Iranians were by nature a practically minded people, they had to struggle for their very existence in a land of extreme heat and cold, and had perpetually to be on the defence against the robber hordes of the steppe. When metaphysical issues arose, however, in Zoroastrianism, evil was ascribed either to Ahura or to a proto-Spirit. But as to how this

Spirit of evil came into being there was no sure conclusion.   Like other cosmogonies, the Iranian is
neither consistent nor complete, and shows signs of
development and alteration during the periods covered
by the literature.

First of all we meet with what has been called the
'monotheistic dualism' of the Gathas, followed by
the pure dualism of the later Avesta.   Then came
the Zervanite view that 'Boundless Time' was the
originator of the two world-principles.   Finally, there
is the Gayomartian theory that evil was derived from
an unrighteous thought in the mind of Ahura, who
once wondered whether it would be possible for him
to have an opponent, and what he would be like.
The Zervanites and Gayomartians were sects of the
fourth and fifth centuries A.D.   The Zervanites, who
were the larger and more important sect, originally
held that Eternity was an Attribute of Ahura, but
later taught that Zervan was the parent of both
Angra Mainyu and Ahura.   Our knowledge of this
sect is fragmentary, since all that is known of them is
from statements of non-Zervanite writers, who record
conflicting accounts of their tenets.   Some say that
Zervan desired offspring for ten thousand years only,
and that Ahura was conceived for his pleasure.   But
Angra Mainyu came into being as the twin brother
of Ahura.   Angra Mainyu, like Jacob, managed to
supplant his brother at birth, and gain great power.
Zervan hated Angra for his ugliness, yet as he had
vowed sovereignty to his firstborn, allowed him this
for nine thousand years.   The Zervanites were divided
regarding the function of evil.   Some held that it was
co-eternal in Zervan, whilst others said that evil had
been introduced as a necessary element in life, and

partly to prove to Ahura that he was not omnipotent. Others regarded evil as an accident, and under Christian influence postulated the Evil One to be a fallen Angel. The Zervanites had a strange cosmogony of their own, and held a fatalistic doctrine of man. In addition, they maintained that the planets were really chained demons, whilst the constellations were friendly to man. This latter was due to Babylonian astrological influence. The power of the Zervanites was never extensive, and they lapsed finally into Mithraism.

The Gayomartians are known chiefly through a Muslim historian who also gives an account of the Zervanites, who, faced with the same problem as the Zervanites, declared that light was eternal and darkness created. Their doctrine accords with the majority of modern Parsi teaching, that Angra Mainyu is opposed by Spenta Mainyu rather than by Ahura Mazdah. For them, Ahura was the sole creator, but within him are two faculties or aspects, the good Spenta Mainyu and the evil Angra Mainyu, who fought eternally. The Gayomartians, however, added that a mediator, in the form of an angel, stopped the conflict and brought about peace for a period. During this time Angra Mainyu was to have dominion, but he had to resign his power at the end of seven thousand years. So the Evil One slew the primal Man and Ox. But instead of the man, there grew up a great plant, from which came the first pair of human beings, and in place of the Ox came a host of domestic animals, who lived on after the evil dominion, and formed the beginning of the good creation.

From these strange stories of the beginning of things we now pass on to consider the doctrine of the future of man, and of his deliverance from the present

evil age. In the Gathas, the Prophet had spoken
with no uncertain voice about the future of the world.
We have noted that his teaching was eschatological ;
for his time, his eschatology was extraordinarily
advanced. He believed that the world-process would
be almost immediately consummated, and like the
Hebrew prophets, proclaimed an approaching ' Day
of the Lord,' and a ' Saviour ' of the people. The
Gathic teaching on this subject is found in the forty-
fifth Yasna : ' Whoso therefore in the future lightly
esteemeth the Daevas and those mortals who lightly
esteem him—even all others save that one who highly
esteemeth him—unto him shall the holy Self of the
future Saoshyant (Deliverer), as Lord of the house,
be friend, brother, or father, O Mazdah Ahura ' (verse
2). From this it is implied that the Prophet himself
will be the future Saoshyant, though the later Avestan
Books look to a subsequent Deliverer or Deliverers,
of the line of Zoroaster.

The consummation of the world is described in the
Gathas as ' the last turning point in creation ' (Ys.
XLIII, 5). The Deliverer would come, and trial by
ordeal awaited all men. A flood of molten metal
would be poured out in which the wicked are burnt
up, but the righteous remain unscathed. Then would
the kingdom of Ahura Mazdah be established, and
given to those who have not followed the Druj, but
rather have delivered him over to the creator : ' So
when there cometh the punishment of these evil ones,
then, O Mazdah, at thy command shall Good Thought
establish the Dominion in the Consummation, for
those who deliver the Lie, O Ahura, into the hands
of Right ' (Ys. XXX, 8). Then would the righteous
not lose their reward—' they that get them good

name shall be partakers in the promised reward in the fair abode of Good Thought, of Mazdah, and of Right ' (Ys. XXX, 10). The Gathas hold that evil cannot be undone, but may be counterbalanced by good deeds, which are the sinner's only hope. There is practically no place for repentance or pardon in Zoroastrian theology which taught salvation by works, every man working out his own salvation. There is no doctrine of atonement. It was believed that there existed a sort of Domesday Book, in which the merits and demerits of each individual were recorded, and accordingly rewards and punishments would be meted out, chiefly of a material nature. We meet nothing parallel to the Indian desire for man's supreme reward to be cessation from all things sensual or material.

For Zoroaster himself, the term Saoshyant included his disciples, who with him were called ' Saoshyanto.' The Prophet thought that through his own work and his followers a new kingdom of righteousness would be brought in, and all evil overcome. But the kingdom did not come : the Parsis therefore taught that three Deliverers would have to come in succession to the Prophet before the consummation could be accomplished. The first of these would be named Ukhshyat-ereta (Increaser of Right) ; the second, Ukhshyat-nemah (Increaser of Worship), would prepare the way for the third, Astvat-ereta (Incarnate Right), who is the final and greatest Saoshyant. The Bundahish was bold to fix the date of his advent ; he would be born in the year A.D. 2341, and when fifty-seven years old would bring in the Restoration (A.D. 2398). Thus many Parsis believe that he is yet to come. This Deliverer is to raise the dead, teach a new revelation,

and inaugurate a Golden Age under Ahura. Evil is
to be expelled from off the face of the earth, and
the ice age which occurred in the days of Yima, will
never again come to pass. The earth is to be made
flat, and become one great plain. The bodily resurrection of all men, which accompanies the appearance
of the Saoshyant, is to bring good and bad alike from
the places where they died. According to one account,
the righteous are to go straight to Heaven, and the
wicked to Hell for three days of torment for their
misdeeds, but afterwards they return to perform
good actions that will wipe away their sins.

The general Pahlavi teaching concerning the consummation of the world postulates Universalism.
The Bundahish says that the Saoshyant will prepare
an ambrosia which would make all men, including the
wicked, immortal. Later Manichaeism, however, held
that the world would be destroyed by a great fire
lasting some fifteen hundred years, yet the heat
would not be sufficiently intense to destroy the wicked,
who would always remain. But such a doctrine does
not tally with the teaching of the more important
Books, which maintain that all would eventually find
bliss, every tongue confess the name of Ahura as God,
and that Hell, Ahriman and his evil Angels would
be annihilated.

Concerning the nature of Heaven and Hell, we
find many interesting conceptions. It seems that the
Gathas assumed that no deed would go without
some kind of reward either of blessing or punishment.
It is hardly likely that the Prophet had worked out
a theory of punishment, yet he did urge strongly
that wrong would not go unpunished to all time.
The fact of sin was so real to him that he felt that

Ahura could not deal leniently with those who had long broken his law—' His burning wrath against intolerable wrong, against the callous cruelty and self-chosen blindness of men who refused his gospel and murdered his faithful people, burned too strongly for him to see any deliverance from the house of the lie.'[1] Thus Zoroaster pictured a punishment that would be ' eternal,' though exactly what is implied by the word so translated is a matter of dispute. Casartelli thinks it means ' perpetual ' rather than ' age-long.' This castigation of the wicked which Zoroaster predicted was not merely of a vindictive nature : its purpose was that evil might eventually be restored to the good creation. Yet the Prophet could not imagine the divine justice satisfied until the last penalty had been exacted. Zoroaster, incidentally, made allowance for a certain class of people, who, like Kipling's *Tomlinson*, were not good enough for Heaven, and not bad enough for Hell—' According as it is with the laws that belong to the present life, so shall the Judge act with most just deed towards the man of the Lie and the man of the Right, and him whose false things and good things balance ' (Ys. XXXIII, 1). The fate of such a man, however, is not conjectured. When Moulton lectured to the Parsis in Bombay, he warned them against setting a lesser emphasis on the reality of sin than their Prophet had done : the greatest sin was not neglect of the ritual code, but selfish action which brings pain on others and which corrupts the human person- ality. Zoroaster realized the perils of such sin so intensely that he declared its punishment must be ' Misery, darkness, foul food, and crying of woe '

[1] Moulton : *The Teaching of Zarathushtra*, p. 51.

7

(Ys. XXXI, 20). Such a torment the soul would
bring upon itself, having found at length its own place.

The Gathas really have two theories of the future
of ' the followers of the Lie,' which were never satisfactorily reconciled. The wicked were either to be
totally destroyed, or to endure long punishment of a
retributive character; which was the Prophet's own
conviction is not known. Perhaps he had no more
definite conviction than an assurance that the pros-
perity of the wicked would suffer a complete reversal
at the hands of God. Thus he taught a simple doctrine,
which was remarkably consistent : there would be a
Heaven of bliss, and a Hell where everything would
be the opposite. The only entrance to Heaven could
be gained through good works done on earth : status
or authority in the worldly existence would confer
no benefit or advantage in the heavenly.

Zoroaster called Heaven the ' House of Song,' the
' Dwelling of Good Thought,' and the ' Kingdom of
Blessings.' Alternately, Hell is given the name of
' House of the Lie,' ' House of the worst Thought,'
or ' Home of the Daevas.' It is probable, however,
that for Zoroaster Heaven and Hell were not primarily
places, but states of mind, to describe which he used
figurative language. Thus the Prophet never seems
to have taken delight in describing purely material
features of the future life, as did Muhammad. Nevertheless, Zoroaster appealed to men that they should
choose good rather than evil that it might be well
with them at the day of the consummation. Though
it would be unfair to say this was the motive of good
action, there is practically no emphasis on ' right
for right's sake.' Zoroaster himself asked Ahura for
a reward in this life, and demanded that he should

be given horses and a camel. He also stated in the Gathas that the believer, who merits the rewards of the future life, would receive two cows in calf, as a foretaste of the blessings to come. Since, however, these benefits were not forthcoming in many cases, Zoroaster was compelled to think in terms of the other world for their fulfilment. From the character of the God he knew, whose Attribute was Asha, the Prophet was convinced that the righteous should not lose their reward, but would dwell in the House of Ahura for ever : ' His (the good man's) dwelling places shall be in thy House, O Ahura ' (Ys. XLVIII, 7). Or again : ' If, O ye mortals, ye mark those commandments that Mazdah hath ordained—of happiness and pain, the long punishment for the liars, and blessings for the righteous—then hereafter shall ye have bliss ' (Ys. XXX, 2).

The Persians taught that all men when they died had to appear before a throne of judgement (Aka). Zoroaster did not define the nature of the trial ; this was amply done by later writers. Ahura Mazdah presided over the court of justice, but a trinity of judges, acting in obedience to the will of Ahura, would give decision. These were Mithra, Sraosha, and Rashnu. Rashnu was generally considered to be first in charge, and he is often portrayed with scales in his hand. He reads the Self of a man, and gives fair judgement according to the evidence of the book of deeds. A Bridge of Decision, called Cinvat, has to be crossed ; this is nine spears length wide for the righteous, but as narrow as a razor edge for the wicked, who fall off into Hell. Cinvat is mentioned three times in the Gathas, and the Prophet may have made use of an ancient Aryan myth concerning the rainbow. From it was derived the Islamic doctrine of the Arch of Al-Sirat. Zoroaster himself would be on the Bridge, and would plead for those whose destiny was uncertain : ' And those whom I impel to your adoration, with these will I cross the Bridge of the Separater ' (Ys. XLVI, 10). We see that the Prophet was responsible for a forensic picture of the judgement, though he made no mention of Rashnu. His conception of the molten flood which would accompany the consummation, must be added. This has proved a difficult doctrine to many who have found it difficult to imagine Zoroaster advocating such cruelty. But Moulton's explanation that the flood was merely a symbol of trial by ordeal, is convincing. Likewise did Paul write, ' Each man's work shall be made manifest : for the day (of the consummation) shall declare it, because it shall be revealed by fire ; and the fire shall try each man's work of what sort it is. If any man's work abide which he hath built thereupon, he shall receive a reward. If any man's work shall be burned he shall suffer loss : but he himself shall be saved ; yet so as through fire ' (1 Cor. III, 13-15).

Cinvat is mentioned three times in the Gathas. It leads to ' Garo Demana,' the Pahlavi ' Garotman,' which is the Paradise of God, where Ahura dwells in realms of light with all the faithful. The later Books maintain, however, that there are four Heavens which have to be passed through before the final abode of the blessed is attained. Those who fall from the Bridge Cinvat descend into a Hell of numberless torments, the nature of which is a matter of much speculation in the later Avestan Books. One tradition says that Hell is the place of complete loneliness.

The wicked will be crowded there as close as hairs on a horse's mane, but each one says, ' I am alone,' and after a day's punishment asks, ' Are the nine thousand years not yet past after which we shall be set free ? ' Apparently the punishment here recorded is not everlasting : it would be abolished when the Saoshyant came. Some hold that Zoroastrianism teaches that there are four Hells, even as there are four Heavens, but this idea is not developed in many of the accounts. Most of the Persian Books agree, however, in placing Hell in the regions of the north.

Later Parsism described the place where those who had been neither good nor bad in this life could be sent—Hamistakan, which was a kind of Purgatory. The word itself means ' in equilibrium.' The Arda-Viraf, a work belonging to the fifth or sixth century A.D., tells of the visit of a Zoroastrian seer to the abodes of the dead, and a detailed account is given of Hamistakan. The seer came to one region of the under-world and inquired what people were doing there. The Angel who was conducting him round replied : ' They call this place Hamistakan, and these souls remain in this place till the Resurrection ; and they are the souls of those men whose good works and sins are equal . . . for every one whose good works are three scruples more than his sins, goes to Heaven ; they who sin in excess go to Hell ; they in whom both are equal remain among these Hamistakan till the Resur-rection. Their punishment is cold or heat from the revolution of the atmosphere, and they have no other adversity.' [1] One man whom the seer beheld in Hell was there not because he had done any wrong, but

1 *Arda-Viraf*, VI, quoted by Casartelli, *E.R.E.*, Vol XI, p. 848.

because he had done no good deeds in his life. Although his body was being consumed, his right foot was not harmed, because with that foot he had once cast a bunch of grass before a ploughing ox. There is nobility in the faith which discerns virtue in such simple actions.

CHAPTER VI

DEVELOPMENTS AND CONTACTS

In this final chapter it remains to give some account of the sects and customs associated with the Zoroastrian faith in its later stages, and to notice a few of its many contacts with other religious systems, especially with Judaism. First of all, the Magi claim attention. The Magi were responsible for introducing a large number of new elements into the religion of Persia, as well as for re-introducing certain old customs and beliefs. They were a priestly caste of great antiquity, like the Brahmans ; and Herodotus says they were one of the six tribes into which Media was divided. The reformation of Zoroaster meant little to them, and their introduction of legalism and alien custom retarded the progress of the true Persian religion. Indeed, almost a new religion was taught by them. Moulton thought that the Magi were originally part of the indigenous population of Media, and thus were neither Aryans nor Semites. This somewhat daring thesis, though not generally accepted, has not yet been challenged with contrary evidence of any weight ; in fact, since the War there has been practically no Iranian research of importance. There were probably other Magi than those who lived in Persia, and it may be that their curious practices which are described by Greek historians were dissociated from Persian Magianism.

The name Magi is found but once in the Avesta :
it may for obvious reasons purposely have been
deleted. Its derivation is obscure, the name may
mean ' helpful,' i.e. to drive away evil Spirits. This
the Magi accomplished, consulting the stars, and
healing the sick through magical formulæ and incanta-
tions—so they claimed. Another theory is that Magi
was a nickname ; many religious bodies have been
known by such (' Quakers,' ' Methodists,' &c., and
even ' Christian '). Others say that the word means
' slave,' a term which may have arisen when the
Magi were driven from the throne of Media. Gautama
the Magus, in the disguise of the brother of the
murdered King Cambyses, seized the throne for a
while, but was soon slain by Darius. Darius used
to hold a festival, called the Magophonia, when
celebrations were made to commemorate the fall of
the Magian king. But very soon the Magi regained
their influence in the land, in religious rather than
in political circles. The adventures of Gautama the
Magian are recorded on the Behistun inscriptions,
which add that Darius rebuilt the sanctuaries which
had been destroyed by Gautama. Although the
Greek writers considered Zoroaster himself to have
been a Magian, there is no real evidence for this view,
which is confidently rejected by Moulton and others
who maintain that the influence of the Magi was
not felt to any extent in Persia until the fifth century
B.C., which would be subsequent to the death of the
Prophet. This is confirmed by a statement of Diogenes
Laertius : ' Xanthos the Lydian says six hundred
years passed between Zoroaster and the invasion of
Xerxes ; and that after him there was a long succession
of Magi, with names like Ostanes, Gobryas, and

Pazates, up to the conquest of the Persians by Alexander.'

The Magi established a hierarchical system in Persia, which was at its strength in the Arsacid dynasty. The chief of the Magi, who considered himself to be in direct succession to Zoroaster, then lived at Balkh, which had become the centre for the priesthood. The Magi also supervised the educational system of the land ; Plato says that even the children of the Persian kings were tutored by them. So powerful did their influence become that Artaxerxes (A.D. 226), issued a decree prohibiting all religious practices other than those taught by the Zoroastrian Magi. A large number of Greeks were thus driven from Persia, and many of their temples destroyed. Both Jews and Christians were also involved in this persecution. But this was probably not through the will of Artaxerxes himself, who was leniently disposed to the Jews : his son Shahpur, however, stirred up hatred against all foreigners. Under Artaxerxes, the Persian Empire grew rapidly, the Parthians were defeated, and a vast territory was unified ; for a while it threatened the power of Rome herself. The Magi were then very prominent in all national affairs, and gathered for themselves great riches from the exaction of tithes. The researches of Dr. Spooner have revealed the important position the Magi held also in India, and some of the practices of the Zoroastrian Magi are reflected in the Mahabharata, one of the great Indian epics.

The Magi were responsible for introducing into Persia the custom of burying the dead on Towers of Silence, or Dakhmas. Though this is the present Zoroastrian mode of burial, it did not originate from

Persia, and the Persians themselves did not use this method until the Sassanian period. Schrader thinks the Dakhmas were imported from Baluchistan, from a tribe known as the Oreitae. The ancient Persians buried their dead, having first covered the bodies with wax. The Avestan doctrine of a resurrection of the body in the form in which it had died—despite the dissolution—would find no use for the Dakhmas. The body was sacred, and would be rejuvenated at the consummation which would follow the advent of the Saoshyant. But the Magian practice represents a very different view. A corpse might defile the earth ; it was therefore exposed to the birds of the heaven, and only the clean bones would be left. The modern Parsis use stone towers and floors, so that the earth itself shall not be corrupted. One reason sometimes offered for the practice of Dakhma burial is that the birds shall carry the body to heaven, but the primary reason is that the elements shall not be defiled.

Greek writers charge the Magi with next-of-kin marriages. That such marriages sometimes occurred is very likely, and Dr. Spooner has traced sister-marriage in the ancestry of Gautama the Magus. Although the Magian priests may have advocated this degrading practice, there is no reference to it in the Avesta, and it has certainly never been generally favoured by the Zoroastrian community. Amongst Avestan literature, the Vendidad is the most representative of Magian teaching, and this is absolutely free from any suggestion of the propriety of next-of-kin marriages. Rather do we find in the Vendidad a highly developed dualistic system which was perhaps the centre of Magian doctrine. The Book of Tobit, though a Jewish work, also contains a considerable amount of Magian teaching, though Casartelli denies that it was written under Magian influence. Casartelli holds that since this Book favours earth-burial and other non-Magian customs, it is really a treatise directed against the Magi, by one who was well acquainted with their tenets. But the Magi had been successful in introducing into Zoroastrianism the very things which the Prophet would have rejected.

Amongst other Zoroastrian sects, mention has already been made (ch. V) of the Zervanites and Gayomartians. To these must be added the Saisaniya, a sect of the eighth century A.D., who, probably under Islamic influence, protested against the drinking of wine, the worship of fire, and next-of-kin marriages. The founder of the Saisaniya, by name Khawwaf, was put to death, and is said to have ascended to Heaven on a yellow horse. Apart from these facts, and that the Saisaniya were a wealthy people who objected to eating the flesh of any animal until it was old, we have no further record of the doings of this strange sect. The practice of fire worship, which was denounced by the Saisaniya, is still found in India to-day. Ideally, as we have maintained, fire is to the Parsi the symbol only of the deity, and a very beautiful symbol. Zoroaster had thus allowed the fire-cults to remain ; his attitude was like that of the author of Ecclesiasticus—' The sun, when he appeareth, bringeth tidings as he goeth forth, is a marvellous instrument, the work of the Most High : at his noon he drieth up the country, and who shall stand against his burning heat ? . . . Great is the Lord that made him ; and at his word he hasteneth his course ' (Ecclus. XLIII). But the thing symbolized once again became subject to the symbol, and in India and Scythia, as well as in Persia, adoration was given to the sun and its fire. The Indians called the fire 'Agni' (cf. Latin 'Ignis') and worshipped it as being used of the deity to take sacrifice up to heaven. But the Persians, who called fire 'Atar,' believed that it attracted the gods down to earth.

The modern practice of fire-cult has been explained on the lines that as man will someday turn to ashes, it is his duty to scatter fragrance through the burning of sweet smelling sandalwood, that his life and death may be blessed. In Parsi temples, various perfumes are sprinkled into the urns in which the fire is kept. The fire is tended five times a day by a priest, or Mobed, who wears a veil over his face lest his breath should defile the sacred flame. His hands also are covered, by gloves, as a like precaution against pollution. Prayers are offered that evil Spirits may be driven away, each time the sandalwood feeds the flames; the Mobed holds the 'Baresman' branch to the nose whilst praying. In many private houses there are also altars where the holy fire is kindled. There are three kinds of Fire Temple, graded according to the amount of purification the fire in them has undergone. The fire of the chief temples (Atesh Behram), which are so constructed to prevent the sunlight falling on the fire and dimming or extinguishing it, is compounded sometimes from sixteen different sources, all elaborately purified. The fire-cult ceremonies are very ancient. Besides the Ezekiel reference noted above, the Greek writers describe them; Strabo tells how the priests in Cappadocia went daily to shrines and sang for an hour before the fire, holding a bundle of twigs (the 'Baresman') and wearing a head-dress which covered the mouth. Zoroastrians only are now allowed in the fire-rooms of the temples, but men and women mix and worship there together. After ablutions and prayer, the worshipper goes to the door of the fire-room, and receives from the Mobed a ladle full of ashes, with which the face is smeared. Prayers such as the Ashem Vohu ('Right is the highest good, so our own rights meet heart's desire when Right attains its heights') may be supplemented with extempore prayers. There are no sermons, and little religious instruction.

During the Sassanian dynasty, Zoroastrianism came into close contact with Manichaeism. It has been held that the dualism taught by Mani was due to Zoroastrian influence : this is stoutly denied by A. A. Bevan, who says that 'the aim of the Zoroastrian is to banish evil from the world, the aim of the Manichaean is to extract from the world that which is good.'[1] Thus Manichaeism has more in common with Buddhism than with Zoroastrianism ; it represents a rival faith rather than a sect of Zoroastrians. Mani was put to death in the year A.D. 274 by the Persian monarch Bahram I, and the rivalry between the two faiths abated, though various Manichaean factions lingered on for a long while.

In the fifth century A.D., Mazdak, a Persian, endeavoured to reform the Zoroastrian religion, by introducing a doctrine of rigid asceticism. He also preached communist theories of property, and advocated drastic measures of social reform. He allowed no beast to be slain for food, and himself lived in the simplest manner. For a while Mazdak was extremely

---

[1] *E.R.E.*, Vol. VIII, p. 400.

successful in his mission, which he claimed was to teach the true faith of Zoroaster. Mazdak, however, together with many of his followers, was treacherously massacred, and the new reformation came to an end.

The Neo-Pythagoreans owed not a little to Zoroastrianism : they taught a doctrine of immortality and dualism which was very akin to Magian belief. There is, in fact, a tradition that Pythagoras himself received his lore from the Magi of Babylon, and the Neo-Platonist leader, Apollonius, came from Tyana, a Cappadocian city in which Persian influence was strong. But the mystical element in Neo-Platonism was certainly not Zoroastrian ; it had probably been adopted from Oriental theosophy. Gnosticism, in its many branches, was also indebted to Zoroastrianism. We may compare Zoroaster's emphasis on Right Thought with the Gnostic theory that redemption was from falsehood and ignorance. But the Prophet had never taught the evil nature of matter, which was central in Gnosticism.

Contacts with Brahmanism, which were of vital importance, especially in the early formative period of the faith of Iran, have been pointed out from time to time in the previous chapters : the two religions are of common Aryan origin. It is probable, however, that Zoroastrianism retained the more essential characteristics of the ancient Aryan religion than did Brahmanism. The ' Brahma,' though possibly a kindred conception to that of Ahura, never became personified in the same way. The Persians were quick to ascribe personality to their deity. The dualistic belief of the Avesta has no parallel in the Vedas which nevertheless abound with the names of demons. Many of the heroes of the Vedas are also the heroes of the Avesta, whilst there is likewise resemblance in the cultus of the two faiths, especially as touching the initiation ceremonies. The Avestan Mithra is the Vedic Mitra, and the worship of this god may go back to a common Sumerian origin. Although Zoroaster ignored him, later teaching exalted Mithra, together with the goddess Anahita, to a position of great importance. The name Mithra means 'compact,' and thus Mithra became the god of contracts and oaths ; he who broke such was the 'Mithra Druj.' The tenth Yasht pays reverence to Ahura and Mithra as gods of like power. Legend told that Mithra had a palace built for him by Ahura on the sacred Mt. Elburz. Mithra had many functions beside being god of contracts : he gave victory to armies, helped the righteous into Paradise, sent down rain from the heavens and light from the sun. He was also regarded as a benefactor to men as he had slain the primeval Bull. With this latter belief may be compared the later Mithraic bull-sacrifice. The Mithraism which was adopted by the Romans in the first century probably was not much influenced by Persian thought, though the Roman Mithras was god of war and of victory.

In modern days, some eleven thousand Gabars, or Zoroastrians who have not migrated to India, still live in a few scattered communities in Persia. But the majority of Zoroastrians are in India. A large number of refugees from the Islamic massacres fled to Surat in the seventh century, and later settled in Bombay, where they still remain. In Bombay there are now about fifty thousand Parsis, most of whom are well-to-do, and educated. Various minor Parsi congregations are found in other cities of India. An old quarrel, dating from 1745, divides the Parsis into two sects, the Kadmis and the Shenshahis, the former of the two incorporating another sect known as the Iranis. The differences between these bodies is largely superficial, the chief object of dispute being the time of observance of the annual feasts. The Iranis are the Zoroastrians who have recently come from Persia, and together with the Shenshahis form by far the largest sect. They celebrate their New Year's Day, which is a great religious festival, in September, whilst the Kadmis keep theirs in August, and have a separate priesthood and temples. There are also Reform and Modernist parties, which are opposed by the Orthodox. Two Parsi scholars of distinction, Professor P. A. Wadia and Dr. Maneckji Dhalla have led a Modernist movement, making protest against the vain repetition of meaningless prayers and customs which were only of value in a primitive community, but as yet have been able to do little in the face of deep-rooted tradition. Professor Wadia says, ' the present-day Parsi grows cold and apathetic towards his creed and ritual and feels that the only things worth living for are the things that belong to his daily avocation, the things that bring him material ease and comfort, that religion is cant and hypocrisy and that the priesthood is a selfish hierarchy of men interested in preserving their own domination.'[1] Perhaps this statement is not unbiassed, yet there is a growing dissatisfaction among the Parsis, and a desire for a closer touch with reality. The exclusive spirit, which caused even the sympathetic Dr. Moulton to describe the Parsis as

---

[1] *Zoroastrianism and our Spiritual Heritage*, p. 55, quoted by Macnicol : *The Living Religions of the Indian People*, p. 263.

'a caste, compassing sea and land to frustrate the making of a proselyte,'[1] is slowly breaking down, but will take many centuries to disappear.

Whatever may be his party, every Parsi wears the sacred girdle, or Kusti, made of seventy two threads, symbolizing the seventy two chapters of the Yasna. All sects, besides celebrating the feasts and fasts of the faith, pay worship at the Fire Temples and offer the sacred Haoma juice, which is drunk sacramentally by the priests, and given as a last consolation to the dying. Initiation rites are long and complex ; the central rite, or Barashnum, incumbent on Mobeds, takes nine days, and is accounted as atonement for such acts as travelling by rail or sea or losing one's headgear ! The ordinary priesthood is divided into two classes, Ervads and Mobeds, but priests of the highest grade are known as Dasturs. The chief priest is called Dastur-i-Dasturan. There is little asceticism in modern Parsism, and the priests are allowed to marry ; many, however, have not the means, as the priesthood is poorly paid. Marriages outside caste are not favoured. Portions of the Avesta are recited daily by good Parsis, some of whom do not know their meaning. In the Parsi Prayer Book, 'portions for the day' are systematically divided, though not according to sequence of context. Each day of the week has its divine patron, and the days of the equinoxes are considered especially sacred to Mithra. A tutor, or confessor of the faith, is kept by many wealthy Parsi families, and is responsible for the religious (and sometimes secular) education of the heir of the household until he is old enough to assume the Kusti, which he will hence forward wear every day of his life.

[1] *The Treasure of the Magi*, p. 128.

8

Despite the existence of the various sects, Parsism now presents a remarkably united body. Gibbon recounts a tradition of the way in which, in the time of the Arsacids, some seventy different sects of Parsism, all contending that they possessed the true teaching of the faith, were reconciled. King Artaxerxes called a council of all the Magi. Some eighty thousand attended. Because it was impossible to control so large a number, he chose forty thousand; but again the number was too great. After various further divisions, seven only remained. One of these, Erdaviraph, was given Haoma to drink: when he awoke from the long sleep that ensued, he declared a divine revelation he had received, and gave authoritative pronouncement on every disputed matter. Whatever the truth of this story may be, there is to-day little dispute in the Parsi community, which abides by the decisions of the Dasturs.

In ethical code, Parsism stands high. The true Zoroastrian abides by the precept of the Vendidad —' Purity is for man, next to life, the greatest good, that purity, O Zarathushtra, that is in the religion of Mazdah for him who cleanses his own self with good actions, words and deeds ' (Vd. V, 21). But ceremonial purity has often supplanted the inward : ' unclean ' things such as hair-clippings and nail pairings are still believed to defile. The bringing of a dog into the presence of a dead body is thought to drive away demons. In practical matters, the Parsis have a lot to teach their brethren in India. They believe in the value of life as a divine gift which must be used according to the divine will. The Prophet had prayed for long life, and this is still desired by his followers, who have confidence in the possibilities of man. Industry is admired by the Parsis : the Vendidad said that whichever of two men rises first at cock-crow, he shall be the first to enter Paradise, and the Dinkart placed much value on honest labour. Zoroastrianism has always placed emphasis on the merits of hospitality, and the Parsis are a very hospitable people. Philanthropy and temperance are also cultivated ; many philanthropic institutions have been endowed in England as well as in India by wealthy Parsis.

We have considered, all too briefly, the great religion of a great people, who in time past offered their rich treasure to the child Jesus. To them is given a noble Prophet and a wonderful heritage. ' But the gold of pure faith is dim with incrustations of ceremonial, of Gnostic speculation and of materialist indifference to religion. The incense is stale, for the prayers of the multitude are in a tongue they cannot understand. The myrrh has only availed to dull the smart of sin. The fire may burn, enthroned and crowned and venerated, in shrines that none but a born Parsi can enter ; but where it should kindle in men's hearts it flickers and burns low. Yet the Treasure is still there, and when they shall turn to the Lord the veil shall be taken away.'[1]

Since this work has been prepared mainly for the use of Christians who wish to study the Zoroastrian faith, it has been thought appropriate, in conclusion, to trace some of the contacts made between the religion of Persia and that of Israel, and through Israel, with Christianity itself. Professor Bousset, in his *Die Religion des Judentums in Neutestamentlichen Zeitalter* has pointed out many features that

[1] Moulton : *The Treasure of the Magi*, pp. 2-3.

Zoroastrianism and Judaism share in common, and holds the conception of Ahura is more akin to that of Jehovah than to any other Eastern deistic conception ; although much may be parallel development only, in some matters there may be vital dependence. If the date of Zoroaster be as early as we have surmised, it is to be expected that his teaching would leave its impress on a great many faiths that were in process of birth. Actually, however, very few of the precepts of the Prophet himself penetrated into other lands ; when the Persian religion began to be assimilated by foreign peoples, the doctrines of the Magi and a very different tradition from Zoroaster's, had taken its place. This later faith was, moreover, more easily adaptable than the Zoroastrianism of the reform.

It is not strange that similar religious ideas should arise in far separated parts of the world ; it would be strange if they did not. Certain moral ideas, in particular, come very near to instinct. Dr. L. H. Mills puts the case concisely by assuming the axiom that 'History not only does, but *must* repeat itself.' And the history of Zoroastrianism has in large measure been repeated in Israel. In the time of the Prophet, there would be practically no possibility of religious interaction between the two faiths. It is chiefly in the Achaemenian (Biblical), Arsacid (post-Biblical) and Sassanian (Talmudic) periods that we look for contacts, and our present concern is with the first of these. The time of the Exile provides the main evidence ; the Jews had entered the Persian Empire, and it is reasonable to suppose that there must then have been considerable interchange of ideas. Scholars once took this for granted, but Gaster, Söderblom, and others have since questioned the thesis that many Jewish religious ideas were born in Persian Babylonia. Yet such scholars do not venture to state where they *did* originate. It must be allowed, however, that some of the leading ideas of the great religions and philosophies of the world are most baffling to trace in origin, and seem void of antecedents. A notable example is the much debated question of the origins of Greek philosophy.

The statements of the Exilic Books of the Old Testament tally with those of many contemporary Persian inscriptions. Often we find confirmation of the historicity of Biblical narratives which, on face value, would be doubted. For instance, the enormous treasure given by Cyrus for the restoration of the Temple, which might well seem exaggerated in Ezra's account, is attested by the Cyrus Vase inscriptions in the British Museum. Cyrus stamped his decrees and edicts on hundreds of clay cylinders which were distributed in various parts of the Empire. The British Museum Vase is a copy of one of these, and was found on a hill in Babylon. A hero of the Exile, Jeremiah, gives the first direct reference to Zoroastrianism in the Old Testament. When Nebuchadrezzar, King of Babylon, took Jerusalem after a siege, among the princes of Babylon who came to the city was Rab-mag (i.e. Chief of the Magi) ; from this it may be concluded that the Magi held positions of importance in Babylon c. 600 B.C.

The evidence of 2 Chronicles, Ezra and Deutero-Isaiah shows the inter-dependence of Babylonian, Persian and Jewish thought. Reigns of Persian kings are even made the basis, in these Books, for the dating of several important landmarks in Jewish history, whilst some passages, apart from their

immediate Jewish authorship, appear as much Persian
as Hebraic. In the last chapter of 2 Chronicles, and
in the first of Ezra, the following remarkable statement
occurs concerning the deeds of Cyrus : ' Now in the
first year of Cyrus, King of Persia, that the word of
the Lord spoken by the mouth of Jeremiah might
be accomplished, the Lord stirred up the spirit of
Cyrus, King of Persia, that he made a proclamation
throughout his kingdom, and put it also in writing,
saying : Thus saith Cyrus King of Persia, All the
kingdoms of the earth hath the Lord God of Heaven
given me ; and he hath charged me to build him an
house in Jerusalem, which is in Judah. Who is there
among you of all his people ? The Lord his God be
with him, and let him go up.' One naturally doubts
whether the great king would have bothered to this
degree over relatively unimportant settlers. Such
an edict, suggests Dr. Mills,[1] might well appear a
patched-up affair, put forward as an inspired utter-
ance in the mouth of Cyrus, by Jews who were
anxious to trace the guidance of Jehovah throughout
all their national history.

The Cyrus Vase inscription, however, substantiates
the Biblical narrative : we read there that ' The great
Lord Marduk (Ahura Mazdah, suggests Mills,) regarded
propitiously the protection, that is, the protector,
of his people, his victorious work, and his righteous
heart, going towards his city Babil as a friend and
as a companion at his side.' This is strangely reminis-
cent, also, of the words of Isaiah, ' Cyrus, whose right
hand have I holden, to subdue nations before him . . .
I have raised him up in righteousness, and I will

---

[1] Whose versions of the Persian inscriptions, in *Zoroaster,
Philo, the Achaemenids and Israel*, are here used.

direct all his ways : he shall build my city, and he shall let go my captives, not for price nor reward, saith the Lord of hosts ' (Isa. XLV, 1, 13). Or again ' Cyrus, he is my shepherd, and shall perform all my pleasure : even saying to Jerusalem, Thou shalt be built ; and to the temple, Thy foundation shall be laid ' (XLIII, 28). Cyrus is the ' anointed ' one of the Lord, ' the man that executeth my counsel from a far country ' (XLV, I, XLVI, II). This description of the goodwill of Cyrus is corroborated by Herodotus, and no idol worship is recorded of him. The Vase inscription says that Cyrus entered Babylon without battle and without bloodshed—' My widely thronging troups came in peace.' Thus was Marduk pleased, as also were the captives, and Cyrus's own estimate of his action surpasses even the Biblical approval. ' Marduk the great Lord made the honourable hearts of the people of Babil incline to me because I was daily mindful of his worship.' Mills concludes that if Cyrus professed such regard for the native gods of Babylon, it is not strange that he looked so favourably to Jehovah, who so much more closely resembled his own Ahura Mazdah. There is nothing unlikely in the Biblical statements of his friendship towards Israel and Israel's God. Cyrus collected the exiles and restored them to their home. Thus in the inscription he prays ' May all the gods whom I have brought into their cities pray daily before Bel and Nabu for long life for me . . . and speak to my Lord Marduk for Kurash (Cyrus) the king who fears thee, and Kambuzi'a his son.' Such a request may be compared with that of Artaxerxes, who asked the Jews to offer sacrifice of sweet savour to Elohim of Heaven and pray for the life of the king and his sons.

The motive of this policy of Cyrus may have been largely political, and, like the Romans, he knew that to interfere with the religion of even a conquered people was to invite trouble. Cyrus, though acknowledging One God, did not wish to incur the wrath of any other gods there might be. So he set himself to restore many old temples and dilapidated sanctuaries throughout the Empire, including the Jewish Temple at Jerusalem. It is therefore most probable that the Jewish and Persian religions were then brought into close contact. During the Achaemenian period, however, very few of the essential practices of Zoroastrianism can be traced with any certainty, and the personal convictions of Cyrus as touching his own faith are difficult to estimate. Darius carried on Cyrus's work. The inscription of Darius, on the famous Behistun rock, substantiates the Biblical statements regarding the enormous extent of the Persian dominion, which embraced over twenty nations. Thus Isaiah well said of Cyrus, that the Lord had holden his right hand to subdue nations before him, and to loose the loins of kings, for this is just what he and his dynasty accomplished. The Chronicles and Ezra record that Cyrus designated his God by the title ' Elohe Hashshamayim,' God of Heaven. This may mean the Iranian Heaven-God, but was a name that could be made applicable to Jehovah, as indeed frequently happened in the post-Exilic literature.

The inscription of Darius makes mention of Ahura Mazdah, and in so doing, presents close parallels with the phraseology of Isaiah. In Isaiah XLV, 12, Jehovah says, ' I have made the earth and created man on it : I. even my hands, have stretched out the heavens,

and all their host have I commanded.' Darius's
inscription reads : ' A great God is Ahura Mazdah,
who made the earth and yon heaven, and made man.'
In another place we read, ' A great God is Ahura
Mazdah who made civilization for man, and who
made Darius king.' Thus Darius claims for himself
the immediate concern of his deity, just in the same
way as Isaiah records of Cyrus that Jehovah had
raised him up to make his power known. Darius
believed that he was ruler of many lands through
divine Right—' As Ahura created this great earth,
he gave it over to me.' Or again, ' Through the
grace of Ahura Mazdah have I placed this earth in
order,' which echoes the words of the Scripture ' All
the kingdoms of the earth hath the Lord God of heaven
given me ' (2 Chron. XXXVI, 23).

The great admiration of the Hebrew writers for the
Persian monarchs seems real ; their eulogistic statements cannot have been prompted by fear. Occasionally, we get a hint that the writers felt they had
gone too far in their praise, and cover themselves
by endeavouring to make quite clear that the good
work of the kings was done for the express glory of
Jehovah, not Ahura Mazdah or any other god. Thus :
' I (Jehovah) will give thee (Cyrus) the treasures of
darkness, and hidden riches of secret places, that
thou mayest know that I, the Lord, which call thee
by thy name, am the God of Israel (and not merely
God of Heaven) ' (Isa. XLV, 3). Mills thinks that
there is here a protest implicit against the claims
that Cyrus might make for his Ahura ; it was for
Jacob and for Israel the chosen of Jehovah that Cyrus
had been called. Isaiah also emphasizes, in con-
tradiction to the inscription of Cyrus, that Jehovah

and none other is the creator and the sustainer of
the world : ' I form the light and create darkness,
I make peace and create evil ; I am the Lord, which
doeth all these things ' (Isa. XLV, 7).

We have noticed previously (in chapter III) this
doctrine of an evil principle within the good God,
taught by Judaism and Zoroastrianism alike : in
the above passage the parallel is very striking, and
the statement of Isaiah may well have been influenced
by the inscription of Cyrus. There is no direct
evidence, however, that Israel was substantially
indebted to Persia for a theory of evil, at least during
the Achaemenian period. Angra Mainyu, the Devil,
is not found on the inscriptions of the time. There
may have been modifications in the Jewish conception
of evil, during the Exile, but they are not of outstanding importance. It cannot be assumed that
because Isaiah and others wrote of Cyrus as a deliverer
of their nation, the Jews adopted any elements of
his religion.

In spite of this, there are so many things shared
between the theologies of Persia and Israel, that
they cannot all be assigned to general community
of ideas. Some of these have been mentioned in other
chapters. It is possible that Zoroastrian thought
gave colour to Hebrew belief in the future life. A
great change is to be found in the Jewish outlook
on this after the Exile. It is difficult, of course, to
state which are the pre-Exilic and post-Exilic narratives
of the Bible, as there is scarcely a Book which does
not contain some Exilic elements. But in so far as
the relevant material can be sifted, the pre-Exilic
doctrine was that no one who died had awakened to
a full, permanent consciousness. The Sheol of the

Hebrews was a dark, dismal place, where, according to the Psalmist, there is no remembrance of God. But the Exile brought new hope for the after-life. A new covenant of individualism was preached, which involved a doctrine of resurrection and of judgement for every man. Ezekiel taught a national resurrection also. His narrative of the ' dry bones,' according to some scholars, may owe debt to Persian thought, at least as regards the image he uses ; Magian theology postulated a resurrection of human beings after their bodies had been exposed to the birds, and the dry bones collected. During the Exile, the old conception of Hades was gradually superseded by the idea of Heaven and Hell, though there is little description of either place in the Old Testament. Persia, however, had long believed in the abodes of bliss and of punishment, and may have passed on ideas about these to the Jews. Later, the Septuagint translators took a Persian word, ' Paradeisos,' (Paradise), which meant a royal park, to convey the idea of Heaven. In Genesis, ' Paradeisos ' is used to translate ' Garden of Eden ' in its original sinless and blissful condition.

Like the Jews, the Persians believed that the soul of a dead man did not leave him for three days : he could not be reckoned *really* dead until the fourth day, when body and soul had separated. In the New Testament account of the raising of Lazarus, it is expressly stated that he had been dead for three days, and was thus entirely beyond recall. Also, it is significant that our Lord rose on the *third* day. Reference may be made to the words of Hosea, ' in the third day he will raise us up ' (VI, 2). The story of Jonah in the belly of the fish three days and three nights offers, it will be noticed, some explanation to Matthew (see Matt. XIII, 40). The issues raised are too complicated to discuss here, yet such parallels with Persian belief cannot be wholly overlooked.

As we have seen, the Persians taught a Messianic doctrine. The Saoshyant, or Messiah, according to Zoroaster, was himself and his disciples. An interesting sidelight on this is the claim now being urged in New Testament scholarship for a ' collective ' use of the title ' Son of Man.'

There is, of course, no evidence for anything here beyond the mere parallel. The Messianic doctrines of Israel and Persia have, however, much in common. The Persian belief that at the advent of the Messiah the earth would be made one great plain, is paralleled by Isaiah—' Every valley shall be exalted, and every mountain and hill shall be made low : and the crooked shall be made straight, and the rough places plain : and the glory of the Lord shall be revealed ' (Isa. XL, 4-5). These words were spoken by one who saw in the triumphs of Cyrus the impending destruction of the Babylonian Empire, which would mean a revolution in the fortunes of the exiles. May we not see here a genuine indebtedness to the promises of the God of Cyrus ? Some hold that the origin of the Jewish Messianic belief came from Persia. This is unlikely. The hope of one who would deliver the nation from its troubles must have been in the minds of the Jews even before the contact with Persia was made. The necessity of a Deliverer arose out of the sense of the Covenant relationship Israel had with her God. God would some day vindicate His cause, and his representative would be of the royal stock of David. The Hebrew Messiah was conceived of in essentially Hebrew ways. The Persian hope of a Saoshyant of the line of Zoroaster would add intensity to the Jewish expectation, and we cannot deny its influence. Yet neither can we assert that such influence was really important : the evidence is too scanty.

The similarity of Jewish and Persian creation and flood stories, their like doctrine of apocalyptic and of a Kingdom of God, and the possibility of a reference to Fravashis in two New Testament passages, have already been noticed. Other coincidences might easily be multiplied, and with them the equally important dissimilarities ; but space forbids. The contacts of Israel with Zoroastrianism may easily be overestimated, but in certain matters, especially during the period that the Jews were in Persian Babylonia, there seems to have been a mutual indebtedness, resulting in a richer legacy of faith for both religions. A late Parsi creed translated by Darmesteter, is cited by Moulton[1] from Söderblom's work *Les Fravashis* : 'I have no doubt as to the good religion of the worshippers of Mazdah, the coming of the Resurrection and the future life, the passing of the Cinvat bridge, the account made during the three nights (of death) of merits and reward, of faults and punishment, the truth of heaven and of hell, the annihilation of Ahriman and the demons, and the destruction of the spirit of evil and the demons, the brood of darkness.' The resemblance of such a creed both to Jewish and Christian belief needs no emphasis. It was fitting, therefore, that the Magi should offer their homage to the great Saoshyant, Who came not to destroy, but to complete.

[1] *Early Zoroastrianism*, p. 289.

APPENDIX I

BIBLIOGRAPHY

BARTHOLOMAE, C. . . Die Gathas des Awesta.

BARUCHA, S. D. . A Brief Sketch of the Zoroastrian Religion and Customs.

BLEEK, A. H. . . . Avesta, from Spiegel's German translation.

BOUSSET, W. . . . Die Religion des Judentums in Neutestamentlichen Zeitalter.

BROWNE, E. G. . Literary History of Persia.

BUCH, M. A. . . . Zoroastrian Ethics.

CASARTELLI, L. C. . La Philosophie religieuse du Mazdéisme sous les Sassanides.
La Religion des rois achéménides d'après leurs inscriptions.

CLEMEN, K. . . . . Religions of the World.

CUMONT, F. . . . Les Mystères de Mithra.
Textes et Monuments figurés relatifs aux Mystères de Mithra.

DARMESTETER, J.
and MILLS, L. H. Avesta, translation. In the *Sacred Books of the East*.

DHALLA, M. N. . . Zoroastrian Theology.

FRAMJI, D. . . . . History of the Parsis.

GEDEN, A. S. . . Studies in the Religions of the East.

GEIGER, W. . . . . Civilisation of the Eastern Iranians in Ancient Times.
Grundriss der iranischen Philologie (with A. Kuhn).

GIBBON, E. . . . . Decline and Fall. Vol. I.

HARLEZ, C. DE . . Des Origines du Zoroastrianisme.

HARNACK, A. . .	Manichaeism. Article in *Encyclopaedia Britannica*, IX.
HAUG, M. . . .	Essays on the Religion of the Parsis.
HOPKINS, E. W. .	The Religions of India.
HYDE, T. . . .	Historia Religionis veterum Persarum eorumque Magorum.
JACKSON, A. V. W. .	Zoroaster the Prophet of Ancient Iran. Zoroastrian Studies. Persia, Past and Present.
KARPADIA, S. A. .	The Teachings of Zoroaster and the Philosophy of the Parsi Religion.
KELLETT, E. E. .	A Short History of Religions.
LABOURT, J. . .	La Christianisme dans l' empire perse sous la dynastie sassanide.
LAING, S. . . .	A Modern Zoroastrian.
LEHMANN, E. . .	Zarathushtra.
MACNICOL, N. . .	The Living Religions of the Indian People.
MALCOLM, N. . .	Five Years in a Persian Town.
MENANT, D. . .	Les Parsis.
MILLS, L. H. . .	Zoroaster, Philo, the Achaemenids and Israel. Avesta Eschatology compared with the Books of Daniel and Revelations. The Hymns of Zoroaster.
MISTRI, R. H. . .	Zoroaster and Zoroastrianism.
MODI, J. J. . . .	The Religious System of the Parsis.
MOULTON, J. H. .	Early Zoroastrianism. The Treasure of the Magi. Early Religious Poetry of Persia. The Teaching of Zarathushtra.
OLDENBURG, H. .	Religion des Veda.
PERRON, A. DU .	Zend-Avesta, Ouvrage de Zoroastre.
RAPP, A. . . .	The Religion and Customs of the Persians and other Iranians, as described by Grecian and Roman Authors.
SANJANA, D. P. .	Zarathushtra and Zarathushtrianism in the Avesta.

SCHRADER, O. . . Prehistoric Antiquities of the Aryan Peoples.

SÖDERBLOM, N. . . La Vie future d'après le Mazdéisme. Les Fravashis. The Living God.

SPIEGEL, F. . . . Eranische Alterthumskunde.

TIELE, C. P. . . The Religion of the Iranian Peoples.

WADIA, A. S. . . The Message of Zoroaster. Zoroastrianism and our Spiritual Heritage.

WEST, E. W. . . Pahlavi Texts. In the *Sacred Books of the East.*

WILSON, J. . . . The Parsi Religion.

WOLFF, F. . . . Avesta.

Articles by Geldner, Meyer, &c., in the *Encyclopaedia Britannica* are also valuable, and comprehensive accounts of many aspects of Zoroastrianism are to be found in Hastings' *Encyclopaedia of Religion and Ethics,* as also in the introductory chapters of the *Sacred Books of the East.* See also article on Zoroastrianism in *Religions of the Empire,* edited by W. Loftus Hare.

APPENDIX II

INDEX OF NAMES

ALSO AVAILABLE FROM THE BOOK TREE

PISTIS SOPHIA: A Gnostic Gospel, translated by G.R.S. Mead. The Gnostics were part of early Christianity and were composed of a number of mystical sects. This was one of their gospels. Virtually all Gnostic teachers were persecuted and their documents destroyed because the Church needed a uniform set of beliefs to operate under. Only now have we begun to better understand these early Christian mystics. This work remains an important milestone in Gnostic research, on par with Nag Hammadi, and should be part of any   serious study. It tells the story of how we, as spiritual beings, have fallen into the world of physical creation. The soul is asleep here, bogged down in physical surroundings, unaware of our true nature. The purpose of Pistis Sophia is to awaken us, and to aid in the process of spiritual freedom. **400 pages • hardcover $55.00 • softcover $27.95**

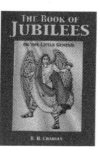

THE BOOK OF JUBILEES, Translated by R. H. Charles. This rare and important holy book sheds new light on Judaism and early Christianity. It was written sometime between 250 BC and AD 100 by one or more Hellenistic Jews, and reflects a form of Jewish mystical thought at around the time of Christ. It retells much of the Old Testament story, but includes additional material not mentioned in the Bible. It also relies heavily on *The Book of Enoch*, which was, like this book, translated from the Ethiopic text. It covers Adam and Eve, the Fall of Man, Cain and Abel, the fall of the angels and their punishment, the deluge foretold, the ark and the flood, the tower of Babel and confusion of tongues, evil spirits, corruption of the human race, God's covenant, the Messianic Kingdom, Jacob's visions, prophetic dreams, and Moses, among other interesting topics. **224 pages • paper $18.95**

THE LOST BOOKS OF THE BIBLE OR THE APOCRYPHAL NEW TESTAMENT, assembled by William Hone. Translated by William Wake and Jeremiah Jones. First published in 1820 under the title The Apocryphal New Testement. These documents were written soon after the death of Christ, during the early days of Christianity. Yet when the Bible was compiled near the end of the fourth century, these texts were not included and were suppressed by the church. **295 pages • 6 x 9 • paper • $24.95**

THE BOOK OF ADAM AND EVE or The Conflict of Adam and Eve with Satan, Translated by Rev. S.C. Malan. This book reveals the life and times of Adam and Eve after they were expelled from the Garden of Eden, up to the time when Cain killed his brother Abel. It covers where they went, where they lived, and their various troubles and temptations, including those coming from Satan. This is an interesting book because it provides one with more information to work with beyond the standard Biblical account. The work includes a number of helpful notes by the translator, issued for clarification, and they appear consistently throughout the text. **256 pages • 6 x 9 • paper • $21.95**

To order call **1.800.700.TREE** 24 hrs. OR visit **www.thebooktree.com**